BEFORE YOU DO MAGIC

ABOUT THE AUTHOR

Donald Tyson is an occult scholar and the author of the popular, critically acclaimed Necronomicon series. He has written more than a dozen books on Western esoteric traditions, including *Tarot Magic*, and edited and annotated Agrippa's *Three Books of Occult Philosophy*. Donald lives in Nova Scotia, Canada.

BEFORE YOU DO MAGIC

TRAIN YOUR MIND TO AWAKEN OCCULT SKILLS

DONALD TYSON

WOODBURY, MINNESOTA

First Edition
First Printing, 2025

Cover design by Shira Atakpu
Interior art by Llewellyn Art Depatment

Library of Congress Cataloging-in-Publication Data
Names: Tyson, Donald author
Title: Before you do magic : train your mind to awaken occult skills / Donald Tyson.
Description: First edition. | Woodbury, Minnesota : Llewellyn Publications, [2025] | Includes bibliographical references and index. | Summary: "Provides twelve chapters that each cover a different topic or type of occult skill-such as concentration, meditation, scrying, astral travel, and aura manipulation-and why it is necessary for better magic. Within each chapter are ten exercises to help develop the corresponding topic or skill"— Provided by publisher.
Identifiers: LCCN 2025033798 (print) | LCCN 2025033799 (ebook) | ISBN 9780738781365 paperback | ISBN 9780738781907 ebook
Subjects: LCSH: Magic | Meditation | Crystal gazing | Astral projection | Aura
Classification: LCC BF1611 .T959 2026 (print) | LCC BF1611 (ebook)
LC record available at https://lccn.loc.gov/2025033798
LC ebook record available at https://lccn.loc.gov/2025033799

Llewellyn Publications
A Division of Llewellyn Worldwide Ltd.
2143 Wooddale Drive
Woodbury, MN 55125-2989
www.llewellyn.com

Printed in the United States of America

GPSR Representation:
UPI-2M PLUS d.o.o., Medulićeva 20, 10000 Zagreb, Croatia
matt.parsons@upi2mbooks.hr

ALSO BY DONALD TYSON

Incantations and Enchantments (2024)

Essential Tarot Writings (2020)

Kinesic Magic (2020)

Tarot Magic (2018)

Serpent of Wisdom (2013)

The Demonology of King James I (2011)

The Dream World of H. P. Lovecraft (2010)

The 13 Gates of the Necronomicon (2010)

The Fourth Book of Occult Philosophy (2009)

Runic Astrology (2009)

Grimoire of the Necronomicon (2008)

Necronomicon Tarot (with Anne Stokes) (2007)

Soul Flight (2007)

Alhazred (2006)

Portable Magic (2006)

Familiar Spirits (2004)

Necronomicon (2004)

1-2-3 Tarot (2004)

The Power of the Word (2004)

Enochian Magic for Beginners (2002)

Tetragrammaton (2002)

The Magician's Workbook (2001)

Sexual Alchemy (2000)

CONTENTS

INTRODUCTION
OPENING YOUR MIND

All magic originates in the mind. Most of the time, it is also expressed outwardly in the form of words, gestures, and actions, but these external aspects are of secondary importance. Magic is initiated in the imagination on the astral level by using mental skills such as visualization, symbol manipulation, emotional control, concentration, and the focus of the will. Physical actions such as the performance of rituals or the making of charms help provide a stable framework for magic, but without the initiating actions of the mind, in themselves they are powerless. The magic done inside your head energizes the magic performed in the outer world using ritual instruments, pentacles, talismans, and other physical materials.

For some reason, people tend to believe they can do magic with no mental preparation or conditioning. Maybe it comes from watching television and movies, in which magic is presented as something anyone can do with no training. They don't make this assumption about any other human activity. They don't assume they can climb El Capitan without skills in rock climbing. They don't think they can swim across the English Channel without learning how to swim. They don't believe they can play a violin concerto without music lessons or dance a waltz without practice. But they think they can cast a spell without ever doing a single exercise to condition their minds, just by mechanically following the steps outlined in a grimoire. It doesn't work that way.

The good news is that the mind can be trained to work magic in the same way the body can be trained to increase physical strength and build muscle mass. In both cases, the rewards are automatic. When you lift weights regularly, you will become stronger and your muscles will get bigger. There's no way to avoid this; it just happens. In exactly the same way, when you practice the exercises in this book regularly, you will acquire the skills needed to work magic. This happens automatically.

Yes, these exercises take some time and mental effort, but surprisingly less of each than you might think. They can be done in fifteen minutes, and they are not complicated or difficult. Too much practice for too long a period can actually do more harm than good, because it tires the mind and tends to provoke depression and frustration. The key factors for success in these exercises are a serious attitude and regular daily practice. After a few weeks, or in the case of some exercises, only a few days, you will notice a difference in your perception of reality. Meaningful coincidences (Carl Jung called these *synchronicities*) will begin to occur in your life. You will find the books and tools you need to work magic, and you will meet the people you need to meet to further your progress. This will happen in ways that seem nothing short of miraculous.

As you practice, spiritual beings will start to notice you and take an interest in your life. This is extremely important, because no mastery of magic is possible without the guidance of a tutelary spirit. Such teaching spirits craft for each magician a unique system of magic tailored to the magician's needs and abilities. One of the great difficulties in first trying to learn magic is how to make contact with your tutelary spirit. Regular performance of the exercises in this book will accomplish this goal. The average person is largely dark on the astral plane and goes unnoticed by spirits. As your occult skills develop, your mind lights up on the astral plane and burns as bright as a star. This will guide your teaching spirit to you.

Each chapter in this book treats a different discipline of the mind that is necessary for working effective practical magic. After background information concerning the discipline is presented, ten exercises are given that are specifically designed to build skill in this area of mental occult development. Collectively, they will provide you with the necessary mental conditioning to successfully perform any style of magic you may later choose to adopt. They are just as useful for witches as they are for necromancers. It doesn't matter if you are a druid, a member of the Golden Dawn, or a chaos magician—these exercises will serve you well, because the mental skills they develop are of universal application.

You will discover that many of the exercises in this book are complete mini-rituals in their own right and can be worked to achieve specific practical goals in your life. You should experiment to find those exercises you need to best develop your own innate occult abilities and to achieve your desired purposes. We all have different strengths and weaknesses. Some exercises may prove more beneficial to you than others. Don't be afraid to devote more of your time to those that give you the best results.

Another thing: don't be intimidated by the sheer number of exercises—it is not necessary to do them all. The reason I provide so many is to give you a choice. If you find an exercise difficult or unhelpful, move on the next. You can always come back to the exercises you skipped at a later date, if you decide to do so. I believe that all the exercises are useful or I would not have included them, but not everyone will react to every exercise in the same way. Find those that work best for you and practice them. The more you practice, the more benefit you will gain from them.

Readers familiar with my book *Kinesic Magic* (Llewellyn, 2020) will recognize that the physical postures used in some of the exercises are simplified versions of postures described in that book. In the present work, I did not wish to overload you with too much complexity. Although these exercises are simple and easy to perform, they are quite effective. Those wishing to delve more deeply into the magic of physical gestures and postures should study *Kinesic Magic*, which lays forth a complete system of magic by means of body positions and movements.

The skills you will learn from the exercises in *Before You Do Magic* are what separate a true magician from someone who merely goes through the motions. All magic is worked in the mind and the heart before it is expressed through the body or by ritual instruments in the outer world. Open yourself to this inner realm of magic and master its secrets, and all its outward forms will seem like child's play.

OCCULT SYMPATHIES

Learning to do magic is all about making connections. Magic works by linking one thing to another. These links are known as sympathies, and the magic that relies on them is called sympathetic magic. This is usually considered only one branch of magic, but if you look deeper into how magic works, you will find that all kinds of magic, even spirit evocation, depend on occult sympathies. You can't do magic without linking things together.

For example, if we wish to summon a spirit using conventional methods, we need to know the spirit's name. That's one link. Then we need to create a graphic symbol that represents the spirit, called a sigil. This is usually based on the spirit's name or its function, and that's another link. We draw or inscribe the sigil onto the surface of some appropriate object or material in harmony with the nature of the spirit—that's another link. What we do to the sigil in a dramatized ritual way is then done to the spirit by the sympathy the sigil has with the spirit. We can strengthen the sigil by inscribing names of power on it, thereby linking these names and the powers they represent to the spirit, and by performing our ritual to summon the spirit at an astrologically auspicious time—yet another link.

The concept of sympathetic magic was set forth in *The Golden Bough* (1890), a book by Sir James Frazer, one of the leading anthropologists of his time. At the beginning of the third chapter of his great work, he wrote,

> If we analyze the principles of thought on which magic is based, they will probably be found to resolve themselves into two: first, that like produces like, or that an effect resembles its cause; and, second, that things which have once been in contact with each other continue to act on each other at a distance after the physical contact has been severed. The former principle may be called the Law of Similarity, the latter the Law of Contact or Contagion. From the first of these principles, namely the Law of Similarity, the magician infers that he can produce any effect he desires merely by imitating it: from the second he infers that whatever he does to a material object will affect equally the person with whom the object was once in contact, whether it formed part of his body or not.[1]

THE POPPET

The classic example of sympathetic magic is the poppet, which is often wrongly called a voodoo doll. It was not used in the Haitian religion of Vodoun but in traditional European witchcraft. This is a doll made by a witch to represent a particular individual. It is

1. James George Frazer, *The Golden Bough,* abr. ed. (New York: Macmillan, 1927), 12.

usually formed out of wax or clay or carved from wood, but it can be made of any material.

The doll does not need to resemble anyone very closely, but it is linked to a person by inscribing the name of the individual on its body and by embedding into it bits of hair, excrement, blood, or nail clippings from the person. Sometimes the doll is dressed in doll clothes that are made from a garment stolen from the person for whom it was made. The doll may also be baptized in the name of the one it represents.

In these ways, an occult sympathy is created between the doll and the person, and once this has been achieved, what is done to the doll has repercussions on the person. For example, if a pin is thrust into the doll's right knee, the person feels a pain in their right knee. This kind of malicious magic is to be deplored, but it was widely used throughout the history of Western magic, and it very clearly illustrates the role of occult sympathies.

TWO PRINCIPLES OF SYMPATHETIC MAGIC

We do not need to rely on ritual robes, tools, substances, or objects of any kind to establish these sympathetic links. We can form symbolic linkages in our minds by using visualization, concentration, willpower, controlled breathing, incantation, and ritual dramatization. In mental magic, the symbols you visualize take the place of charms, incense, candles, or other materials, but it all still works on the ancient principles of occult sympathy.

What are those principles? There are two of them, as defined by Frazer in the preceding quotation. The first is that magic functions through contact, or what Frazer called "contagion." When two things touch or even lie close, they become occultly linked. This is why clothing taken from a person can be used in traditional magic to affect that person. Anything owned or used by someone is occultly linked to them and can be used to manipulate them, either for benevolent or malicious purposes.

The second principle is similarity. A magic link exists between things that are not physically joined but that have similar qualities. Red ink can, and often does, substitute for blood in ritual work because the colors of red ink and blood are similar. In astrology, the planet Mars governs conflicts and warfare on Earth when it is in power positions in the heavens, such as rising in the east or at the zenith, because the god ruling the red planet, the Roman god Mars, is a god of war, an activity in which blood is shed. Here we have the similarities between the color red, blood, warfare, and the god of war, which enable the planet Mars to be used in magic to influence conflicts.

If you consider the poppet, you will see that it is effective as a magical device because it uses both the principle of contact and the principle of similarity. By forming the hair of the doll's head from hair taken from the person it represents, the magical principle of contact is brought into play, and by inscribing the name of the person on the doll and baptizing it in that name, the principle of similarity is activated, because both the person and the doll then have the same name.

These sympathetic links are activated by visualizing in the mind the achievement of the ritual purpose and by dramatically representing with motions of your hands and body the fulfillment of the purpose you wish to achieve. Incantation can be used to more powerfully focus your concentration on the intended goal of the magic as you enact its realization in a ritual manner.

All this would be to no avail without the power of your will, which is used to direct and impel occult energies like a kind of psychic pump. Without willpower, you could not move these forces, which may be visualized as colored streams flowing through the air or through the human body. By the use of gestures, we define and create the channels these occult forces flow along; by visualization, we imagine the flowing of these forces; and by the power of will, we pump those energies through the channels we have created.

BREATH AND BLOOD

Controlled breathing can be used to assist in moving, directing, and focusing these energies. In the next chapter, we will examine controlled breathing in more depth. The breath is considered by occultists to be one of the two primary seats of vital essence in the body, the other being the blood. When we inhale, the occult virtue in the air that fills our lungs is transferred to the blood. In men, the virtue in the blood is most highly concentrated in the semen; in women, it is concentrated in menstrual blood. The natures of these two types of blood virtue are quite different, however. Semen has an energizing, initiating force that is almost brutal, whereas menstrual blood in past times was generally considered to be baneful.[2]

Both breath and blood have been extensively employed in magic all around the world since the most ancient times, but the use of blood is generally to be avoided since it involves releasing it from your body or the body of another living being, which is unnecessary. The controlled use of the breath is sufficient for manipulating occult energies. In my own work, I never use blood

2. See Pliny the Elder on this topic. *The Natural History of Pliny*, trans. John Bostock and H. T. Riley, vol. 2 (London: Henry G. Bohn, 1855), 151. See also Cornelius Agrippa, *Three Books of Occult Philosophy*, ed. Donald Tyson (St. Paul, MN: Llewellyn Publications, 1993), 123.

magic. I advise you to avoid it, especially since fresh blood can attract spirits of a malicious nature.

BUILDING SYMPATHETIC LINKS

As you perform the concentration and visualization exercises given later in this book and meditate on the occult forces of Western magic, be aware that you are building linkages not only in your subconscious mind but throughout your physical nervous system. You will feel various parts of your body and brain activated during these exercises. This is a normal part of the work, as these sympathetic linkages cease to be purely imaginary and become real. Do not be afraid of these sensations, even though they can feel strange at times. They indicate that you are making progress.

You may feel a tingling in different parts of your body, or you may feel heat or coolness. Sometimes one or more of your muscles will begin to twitch for a time. You will feel energy flowing along the nerve pathways of your body, up your spine, along your arms and legs to the tips of your fingers and toes. You may even hear phantom sounds such as the tinkling of bells or a humming noise, or occasionally a loud bang that has no cause in the physical world. Such phenomena are normal when you are developing the powers of your mind.

By moving occult forces through your mind and body, you will activate various potent magic abilities, which are different for each person. Among these abilities is the power to scry and the power to heal. Your body becomes your temple and your hands your magic instruments. By invoking these potent forces into yourself, you will be able to cause changes in the world around you. You will come to see that you have the ability to work magic with nothing but your body and mind.

The exercises that follow are designed to attune you to your own natural sympathies and to give you practice in recognizing the natural sympathies of others. The key here is awareness. You should do each exercise at least once, just to experience it. If it feels lifeless or pointless, you don't need to do it a second time. Those that resonate within you should be done repeatedly at the same time of day and in the same location until you have extracted all the benefit you can from them.

EXERCISES FOR CHAPTER 1

Exercise 1.1: Animal Guide

Sit in a comfortable chair in a quiet room with the light dimmed. Close your eyes. Consider the animal that best represents your inner essence. Don't choose a large, strong beast automatically, but let your thoughts roam over a wide range of beasts, birds, and other living creatures until you feel a sense that you have found the one that most honestly expresses the aspirations of your true self. The key here is honesty. Not everyone's animal guide is a bear or a tiger. It will come into your thoughts and present itself to you—do not reject it.

Consider this creature in your imagination for a few minutes, watching it move and turn and run in your mind. Approach it and engage with it. Imagine its response to your presence and your extended hand. If the animal allows it, stroke it or pat it gently. Thereafter, whenever you feel nervous or afraid, think of this creature and make it be present in your mind, and it will take away your fear and give you strength.

Open your eyes to end the exercise, which should be repeated numerous times to strengthen the bond.

Exercise 1.2: Personal Space

Go to the place where you feel the most comfortable and at home. It may be a room in your actual home or a place outside it, such as a grove of trees or the seashore. Walk around the place and examine one by one the features of it and the objects present in it. Try to understand why this place makes you feel so much at ease and gives you such a strong sense of belonging.

Close your eyes and stand still, but continue to feel the space around you. Be conscious of its features. Be aware of the sounds and the warmth or coolness on your skin. Absorb the atmosphere of the place deep into yourself. Repetition of the exercise will forge a bond between you and your special place. When you feel depressed, confused, or unhappy, shut your eyes and return to this place in your mind to receive its comfort.

Open your eyes to end the exercise.

Exercise 1.3: Color Meditation

This is a good exercise to do when you feel tired, either mentally or physically. Filling your imagination with your favorite color will tend to restore your energy reserves and refresh your mind.

Find an object that is colored with your favorite color and hold it in your hands. Sit in a comfortable chair and gaze at the object as you turn it slowly in your hands. Be aware of the effect its color has on your emotions and general state of being.

Close your eyes. Flood your mind with that same color on a featureless background, as though you were looking at a sheet of colored paper so enormous that you can't see its edges. Hold the color in your mind for a minute or so.

To end the exercise, open your eyes.

Exercise 1.4: Scent Responses

For this exercise, you will need to obtain several different kinds of incense, in the form of either cones or sticks. Rose, sandalwood, pine, frankincense, jasmine, cinnamon, lavender, myrrh, and sage are all common scents. Each scent will cause a general response in your unconscious mind that gives rise to a consistent category of thoughts and feelings. This exercise will allow you to become aware of which incense is most appropriate to create the general mood you wish to achieve for different kinds of ritual work.

Light an incense stick or cone on the table next to your chair, sit in the chair, and close your eyes. Keep your mind empty but receptive. Allow images and impressions to arise as you focus your awareness on the smell of the incense smoke. Pay attention to the general trend of the thoughts that arise. Continue in this way for ten minutes or so, then open your eyes to end the exercise. Write down the strongest and clearest impressions that came into your mind while you were breathing the scent of the incense.

The next day, do the same exercise with a different incense. Repeat this exercise for at least several different kinds of incense, and compare your notes. Do not do the exercise twice on the same day. The set of impressions from each type of burning incense must be clear and distinct.

Exercise 1.5: Music Imagery

Start an instrumental piece of music playing. If you wish, you can wear headphones. Classical composers work best for this exercise. For example, you might choose a work by Mozart for one exercise, a work by Beethoven for the next, and a work by Bach for the next. Avoid using songs with words, as the lyrics are too much of a distraction and will conflict with the imagery arising in your mind.

Sit in a comfortable chair in a dimly lit room and close your eyes. Make your mind empty and receptive. As feelings and images arise, be aware of their general tenor and type. Turn your focus not to the music but to your response to the music. When the instrumental has finished, open your eyes to end the exercise and write down the strongest impressions evoked by the music.

The next day, around the same hour and in the same location, repeat the exercise with an instrumental piece from another composer. Take mental note of the images and emotions that arise while the music is playing, and write them down at the end of the exercise. Do this exercise at least a few times with different composers to give yourself some idea of which type of music is useful for creating the particular mood you desire to evoke.

In this way, you can learn which composer and which piece of music gives you energy, which depresses you, which causes conflict and confusion, which calms you, and so on. This knowledge can prove useful in future ritual work.

Exercise 1.6: Personal Symbolic Associations

The goal here is self-awareness. By becoming aware of the symbols that have the most meaning for you and seeking to understand them, you can learn more about what defines and limits you as a person.

Sit in a comfortable chair in a dimly lit room and close your eyes. Begin by making your mind empty and receptive. After several minutes, when you are completely relaxed, call into mind a symbol that you sense expresses an aspect of you as a human being. It can be an actual object or an abstract form, but it must be something with symbolic significance for you. It must have meaningful associations that resonate within you on an emotional level.

Examples of the kind of symbols that might resonate within you are a Christian cross, a pentagram, a rose, a white dove, the peace sign, a unicorn, a sword, a silver chalice, a seashell, a serpent, a balloon, an egg, an oak leaf, and so on.

When you have considered this symbolic object or form for a minute or so and experienced fully the way it resonates within you, allow it to fade into nothingness and choose another meaningful symbol. Consider this for a minute or so, then move on to a third symbol. Do this for half a dozen symbolic objects or forms that have meaningful associations.

To end the exercise, take a few deep breaths and open your eyes.

You may wish to select the most meaningful symbol from the exercise and adopt it as a personal token. For example, if it were a Mustang convertible, you might obtain a small model of a Mustang convertible and place it on your shelf where you can look at it regularly. Visualizing symbols that evoke a positive resonance can be a source of strength and comfort at times of emotional distress or physical danger.

Exercise 1.7: Symbolic Links

Sit in a comfortable chair in a dimly lit, quiet room and close your eyes. Consider someone you know well. Hold that person in your mind for a minute or so. Allow the objects and symbols that best express the true nature of that person to arise in your mind, and consider each at length, turning it over in your thoughts and relating it back to the person under consideration. Do this for half a dozen symbolic objects, then open your eyes to end the exercise.

You now have a deeper understanding of what defines and motivates the person you were contemplating. Write down the name of the person and list the objects that arose in your mind.

These symbolic objects will have power over that person, both for good and for ill, and at some future time, you may wish to make use of them in your magic.

Exercise 1.8: Personal Sigil

For this exercise, you need a sheet of blank paper and a pencil. Place them on a table and sit at the table. Close your eyes and take a few slow breaths to clear your mind. Visualize a blackboard and imagine yourself printing your first and last name in block capitals on the blackboard with a stick of white chalk.

Open your eyes and immediately print your name across the top of the sheet of paper with the pencil using the same block capital letters. Consider the letters of your name. Mentally rearrange the letters into a single symbol by overlapping, rotating, and reflecting the letters.

This process will take some experimentation. Use the pencil to try various combinations of letters. You can use a single line for two or more letters that overlap. Try to connect all the letters together. Continue until you have achieved a symbol that seems satisfying and right and that contains in some partial and overlapped form all the letters in your name.

This is your personal sigil. It represents not only your name but your unique nature. It can be used as a seal when making charms and talismans for your own use. Do not show it to anyone else—it is a private matter. Draw out a more finished version on a blank square of paper and put it away in a safe place for future reference.

At another time, repeat the exercise, but this time create a sigil from the name of another person you know. Let the shape of the sigil express the inner nature of that person. Keep your mind filled with the personality and characteristics of the person while you are forming the sigil. Do the exercise several more times on different days but at the same general time of day and in the same place, and each time make a sigil for a different person. Only draw one sigil during each exercise.

You will wish to keep these sigils in a safe place, as they can be used to exert power over the people they represent.

Exercise 1.9: Guiding Star

On a night when the sky is clear, go out and look up at the stars. Find the star that seems to you the most intriguing, the one with which you feel a personal connection on the deepest level. It should be a star that is bright enough and distinctive enough in its placement in the night sky to recognize at a later time.

Return indoors and use a star atlas to identify that star. It is your guiding star upon which you may make wishes and to which you may direct prayers or other personal communications.

When you wish to commune with your star, go out under the night sky and gaze up at it. Talk to it. Open your heart to it. Be aware that the star is listening to your thoughts.

Avoid choosing any of the planets in this exercise. Take some time to seriously consider with an open and receptive mind the entire night sky. You will find yourself drawn to a star that may not be the brightest or best known but that speaks to you on a deep level. This is a sure indication that you have found your own guiding star.

Exercise 1.10: Magic Name

Sit in a comfortable chair in a darkened room with your eyes closed. Make your mind open and empty. Meditate on what you would be called if your name were to express your true inner identity as a practitioner and student of magic. What descriptive name best suits you, as a magician? Not a name that expresses what you wish you were or would like to become, but the name that embodies your occult identity, the true you that you keep concealed.

A name will arise spontaneously. This is your magic name, which you should keep private and not reveal to others, as it can be used to exert power over you. When you wish to draw out the magician that is inside you to do works of magic, you can voice your magic name to yourself. You can also use it to command familiar spirits. The common, everyday person you think yourself to be could not command them, but the magician you carry inside yourself can do so.

CONTROLLED BREATHING

Breathing is one of the ways you regulate the flow of energy through your body while working magic. Whether you call it chi, ki, mana, orgone, prana, vril, kundalini, the Force, or some other name, the essential potency of magic can be accumulated, concentrated, and projected on the breath. It is the limitless, undifferentiated, universal energy of creation.

The power of the breath has been understood by magicians for thousands of years. It is the central engine that drives yoga, the esoteric system of India. Pranayama is the yoga of controlled breathing, and it may be truly stated that without its practice, the other forms of yoga, such as hatha yoga (the yoga of body postures) have little or no spiritual value.

In the Kabbalah, magic energy is embodied on the breath in the form of Hebrew words of power drawn from the sacred texts of the Torah. Occult power is not only in the written words but in the sounds those words make when expressed on the living breath. The chanting aloud of prayers and mantras has great efficacy in manifesting the intention of a Kabbalistic magician, who is known as a *Ba'al Shem* (Master of the Name).

The magic of the breath is older than recorded history. Long before the yogis of India and the Ba'alei Shem of the Jews made use of the power of breath, shamans were using it in distant regions of the world such as Lapland, Greenland, and Tibet to heal or to kill. Shamans inhaled over the mouths of the sick to take the sickness into themselves, where they could combat and overcome it, or exhaled close to an injured part of the body to blow away the pain and weakness.

John Aubrey in his *Miscellanies*, published in 1696, made mention of the practice of placing the head of a living frog, wrapped in a cloth to keep it from wriggling free, into the mouth of a person ill with the disease known as thrush and holding it there until the frog died.[3] In this way, the disease was drawn from the breath of the sick person into the lungs of the frog, which took the disease upon itself and expired. Sometimes as many as a dozen repetitions were necessary to cure the patient. The practice was still going on in rural England during Aubrey's time, and he himself witnessed it. Such ways of employing the breath in magic are numerous, varied, and to be found throughout the history and literature of the occult.

The breath is used along with visualization, concentration, incantation, ritual dramatization, and the power of the will to draw esoteric energies into the body, to direct them through the body, to concentrate them in specific body centers, and to project them out from the body either to transfer or dissipate them.

GENERAL PRINCIPLES OF THE BREATH

The general principles for the manipulation of esoteric energies on the breath may be stated in a few words. Inhalation is used to draw

---

3. John Aubrey, *Miscellanies* (London, 1696), 109.

energies into the body. Retention of the breath with the lungs filled is used to concentrate them. Exhalation is used to direct the flow of energies throughout the body or to project them from the body. Exclusion of the air with the lungs held empty awakens energies latent within the body.

A long, slow inhalation through the nose, followed by a brief pause, then a long, slow exhalation through the nose is referred to in this work as the *silent breath*. The flow of air should be slow and even, so that it makes no sound. The silent breath is useful for relaxing the body or the mind, for calming the emotions, for focusing intention, for creating a receptive mental state, and for emptying the mind. It can be used at the beginning and ending of the exercises described in this book to make the transition from an ordinary, everyday state of consciousness to the heightened awareness that occurs when doing works of magic.

When you employ the silent breath, be conscious of the movement of your chest and diaphragm and feel the air flowing in and out through your nose. If you cannot breathe through your nose due to some nasal obstruction or a head cold, you can perform the silent breath through your parted lips, provided you make no sound. In this case, be aware of the flow of air over your lips as it warms and cools them by turns.

Retention of the breath occurs when you hold your lungs filled with air. When you hold them empty, it may be termed *exclusion* since it excludes the air from your body. The purpose of these two kinds of breath control is to awaken and concentrate esoteric energy that lies dormant within your body. It is through retention and exclusion of the breath that the cosmic force known in tantra as *kundalini*, the fire snake, is aroused from sleep at the base of the spine.

What you must know about retention and exclusion is that you should never try to make your lungs completely empty or to hold them completely filled with air. Either practice will soon result in fits of coughing and pain, and it may take days or weeks to fully recover if the enthusiasm of the practitioner has been excessive.

When inhaling with retention, a rule of thumb is to fill your lungs about four-fifths of the way, and when using exhalations with exclusion, exhale about four-fifths of the air, keeping a little in your lungs. In this way, you will avoid damage.

Never lock your throat while retaining or excluding the breath. You lock the throat by tightening the muscles of the throat, dropping and pulling the chin inward slightly, and pushing the tongue up and back against the back part of the roof of the mouth. Never do this, because it causes unnecessary strain. Keep your throat relaxed and open, and use the muscles of your diaphragm and chest to hold the air in or out.

The duration of the retentions and exclusions is what awakens esoteric energy within the body. The longer the duration, the more potent the effect. It is best to begin practicing these forms of breath control with short durations. Keep the durations even for both the inhalation and exhalation, and count in your mind slow beats of about a second each. Think of the beats as the ticking of a grandfather clock. You might begin with a retention of three beats, followed by an exclusion of the same duration. After practicing for a time, increase the beats to four, then five, then six, and so on.

Exhalation with exclusion is more potent than inhalation with retention, and it is more difficult since your body will fight for air when you hold your lungs empty for more than a few beats. It will produce a fine, cooling perspiration over the entire surface of your body. This is an indication that you are performing breath exclusion correctly. In yoga, this is known as *pore breathing* because the yogis believe the body is taking in air through the pores of the skin. As you practice, you will feel a kind of yearning sensation throughout all your nerves, both along your spine and to the ends of your fingers and toes. This is another sign of correct technique.

AUDIBLE BREATHS

When moving occult energy on the breath, it is best to make the passage of air across the lips audible as a slight whooshing sound, like the distant sound of wind in the trees. It does not need to be loud, but the sound will help you focus your mind on the motion of the breath and the energies it carries. Purse your lips as though about to whistle to produce this sound.

When drawing energy in on the inhalation, you should make the inhalation audible but the exhalation silent, because you are focusing your mind to the influx of energy into the body. Conversely, when directing or projecting energy on the exhalation, you should make the exhalation audible and the inhalation silent. At times you will wish to pull energy on the inhalation and push it on the exhalation, and when you do this, both the in-breath and out-breath should be audible.

When drawing in and accumulating occult energy, you should not try to do it in the form of a continuous, sustained flow. This is very tiring on the concentration and the mind is almost certain to wander. Instead, use the inhalations of your breath as pulses that carry the esoteric force into your body. When you inhale audibly, concentrate strongly on visualizing the inflow of energy, and when you exhale silently, relax your mind and make it empty. By doing this repeatedly, it is possible to accumulate large amounts of *occult virtue*, as this esoteric energy was called by magicians in past centuries. The mind is rested between each inhalation and does not become fatigued.

The sound you make with your lips during an audible inhalation should be slightly different from the sound you make with an audible exhalation. You can achieve this by changing the shape of your lips and position of your tongue. It is useful to differentiate between the sound the breath makes when you are pulling energy and the sound it makes when you are pushing energy.

VIBRATING VOWEL SOUNDS

Controlled breathing when combined with extended vowel sounds can have enormous power in magic. Greek magicians in the centuries before the time of Christ learned this technique from Egyptian priests while the Greeks were ruling over Egypt, following the conquest of Egypt by Alexander the Great. There are many examples in ancient Greek magic and in the Gnostic texts.

The magicians of the Hermetic Order of the Golden Dawn placed great reliance on extended vowel sounds when vocalizing words of power during their rituals. They called this "vibrating words of power," because the extended vowels cause the chest, throat, roof of the mouth, and nasal cavities to vibrate with a buzzing sensation. Vibrated words boom forth like thunder. Aleister Crowley learned this technique while a member of the Golden Dawn and relied on it throughout his life.

The way of vibrating individual vowel sounds, after the manner of the ancient Greeks, or complete words in the way of the Golden Dawn, is not complicated, but it must be practiced. Stand erect with the shoulders wide and the neck extended upward. Focusing on opening a path all the way from your lungs up your throat and into your mouth and nose. Draw a full breath, and as you exhale evenly, cause the column of air inside your torso to vibrate up and down as you sound one of the vowels A, E, I, O, or

U. Extend the vowel sound on your exhalation, and feel it vibrating in the open channels of your sinuses, in your nostrils, against the roof of your mouth, and deep inside your chest.

The sounding of the vowels must not be blocked or obstructed in any way. It must begin at your diaphragm below your lungs and rise freely until it issues forth at your mouth and nose. It is useful to imagine your chest to be hollow so that the sound can resonate inside you before coming out. When this is done correctly, you feel the sound of the vowels as clearly as you hear it.

You will see how these few general principles of breathing are applied in the practical exercises that follow. The exercises are designed to give you control over your breath. It is impossible to overstate the importance and value of this in the practice of magic.

EXERCISES FOR CHAPTER 2

Exercise 2.1: Silent Breath

This breath is used to clear and still the mind, either for the purpose of preparing for the beginning of occult work or to relax after its completion. It is also good for relaxing the entire mind and body. It must be done without strain. It has a beneficial cooling and cleansing effect.

Stand with your arms at your sides and your feet about four inches apart. Breathe in slowly and deeply through your nose until your lungs are almost full, but not uncomfortably so. Hold the breath without straining or locking your throat for the beat of a second, and then exhale through your nose slowly until your lungs are almost empty. Hold your lungs in this emptied state for another beat. Repeat around two dozen times—the exact number of repetitions is not important, so you do not need to count them.

The inhalations and exhalations should be of the same duration, and the periods when you stop your breath with your lungs almost full or almost empty should be of the same length. Strive for a rhythmic flow of air in and out of your body.

If for some reason you cannot breathe through your nose, part your lips slightly and breath through your mouth. In either case, the passage of air into and out from your body should be completely silent. Try to breathe without making even the slightest sound. If you have asthma, don't worry about wheezing, since it can't be helped. Just strive to reduce the sound as much as you can without strain. Never strain in any breathing exercise.

As you perform this exercise, look straight ahead and focus your gaze on the distant horizon. If you are inside a building or your view is otherwise obstructed, which will usually be the case, imagine that you can see the horizon far away at the level of your eyes.

Your mind should be tranquil and empty. As thoughts arise, gently turn them away and keep your attention on your breathing. Feel the coolness of the air as it enters your nostrils and flows down your throat and into your lungs. Your emotions should be neutral and balanced.

Exercise 2.2: Inhalation with Retention

Stand as before with your arms at your sides. Take a few regular, silent breaths to prepare for the exercise.

The effect of this exercise is to charge your body with oxygen. You may begin to feel light-headed when doing the repetitions—if so, perform the exercise sitting down rather than standing. Use a plain kitchen chair and sit with your back erect and your hands on your knees, feet flat on the floor and around twelve inches apart.

Inhale through your nose. Focus your mind on the cooling effect the inflow of air has on the interior of your nose and throat. Do not overfill your lungs. Count slowly for three beats in your mind during this silent inhalation.

Stop your breath with your lungs mostly filled and retain the air, but do not lock your throat—keep your throat open and relaxed. Use your diaphragm to hold your lungs full. Count slowly for three beats while you retain your breath.

Exhale at the same rate at which you inhaled, counting for three beats in your mind as you gently push the air from your lungs and through your nose. Do not completely empty your lungs.

When your lungs are almost empty, pause for a single beat and begin to draw air into your lungs again for the slow mental count of "one ... two ... three."

The duration of each inhalation, retention, and exhalation should be around three seconds at the start of your practice. As you become more skilled, you can lengthen this duration to four, five, or six seconds. The pause when the lungs are empty should be no more than a second. Repeat this cycle a dozen times or so.

To end the exercise, take several regular silent breaths without retentions to relax your mind and body.

Exercise 2.3: Exhalation with Exclusion

Exclusion occurs when you hold your lungs empty of air for a deliberately extended period of time.

The effect of this exercise is to cleanse the body and awaken energy within it. You will feel this awakened energy moving along your nerves, in the core of your abdomen, in the tips of your fingers and toes, and in your groin.

Stand with your arms at your sides, take a few slow silent breaths, and focus on what you are about to do.

Exhale the air from your lungs while counting to three in your mind. Do not struggle to empty your lungs—there must be no strain.

Hold your lungs almost empty for the count of three without locking shut your throat. Be sure to keep your throat relaxed and open.

Inhale and fill your lungs for the count of three, but do not overfill them.

Hold the air in your lungs for only a single beat, then exhale for three beats as you repeat the cycle.

The durations of exhalation, exclusion, and inhalation must be the same. Take care not to get so out of breath that you are rushing your inhalations. If this happens, you must reduce the duration of your count. As you acquire more skill, you can extend the durations, but always keep them of equal length.

Repeat this cycle around a dozen times. Breathe out and empty your lungs for three, hold your lungs empty for three, breathe in and fill your lungs for three, keep your lungs filled with air for only a single second, and repeat the cycle.

To conclude the exercise, take a few slow, silent breaths and relax your mind and body.

Exercise 2.4: Audible Inhalation

This exercise will accumulate and concentrate vital energy in your body. The difference between this exercise and the preceding exercise is that this one draws energy from the outside into your body, whereas exhalation with exclusion of the breath awakens energy that is already present within your body but dormant.

Adopt a standing posture. Take a few silent breaths and focus your mind on what you are about to do.

Inhale slowly through your mouth for the silent mental count of four, and as you draw the air in, purse your lips so that the air makes a slight whooshing sound, like the sound of wind heard in the distance. The inhalation must be even from beginning to end—the sound should not change in pitch or volume during the inhalation.

Pause for a single second with your lungs filled, then close your lips and silently exhale through your nose for the mental count of four. Pause for a second with your lungs emptied, then repeat the cycle.

As is true for all breathing exercises, you must not strain by trying to exhale or inhale too deeply or by trying to hold your lungs full or empty for too long. If the exercise produces strain, you must adjust it until the strain is gone.

Repeat the cycle of audible inhalation through the mouth and silent exhalation through the nose a dozen times or so. If your nose is obstructed, exhale silently through your mouth.

To conclude the exercise, perform a few regular silent breaths and relax your mind.

Exercise 2.5: Audible Exhalation

This exercise will release energy from your body. It can have a pleasant soothing effect, especially if you are tense or keyed up in some way, either mentally or physically. It can be useful to perform it just before going to bed for the night if you have trouble sleeping.

In a standing posture, take a few silent breaths to calm your thoughts and focus on your purpose.

Exhale through your mouth as you count four in your mind. Purse your lips so that the air flowing out of your mouth makes a regular, sustained whooshing sound. It does not need to be loud, but you must be able to clearly hear it. You should shape your mouth so that the sound is slightly different from the sound of inhalation you made in the last exercise.

Hold your lungs empty for a second, then close your lips and silently breathe in through your nose while counting slowly to four in your mind. The duration of the audible exhalation and silent inhalation should be the same. Pause for a second with your lungs full, then repeat the cycle.

Do this audible exhalation through the mouth and silent inhalation through the nose a dozen times or so. Stop if you find yourself becoming dizzy—this applies to all the breathing exercises. If you find that you cannot do the exercise without becoming dizzy, try doing it while sitting on a kitchen chair with your feet flat on the floor and your hands resting on your knees.

End by taking a few silent breaths to relax your mind.

Exercise 2.6: A-O Breating

This exercise can be used as a meditation on God, on your personal spiritual guardian, or on your higher self.

The A represents Alpha, first letter of the Greek alphabet, and the beginning; the O represents Omega, final letter of the Greek alphabet, and the end. This formula was used in the biblical book Revelation to stand for the Supreme Creator: the Alpha and the Omega, the first and last, the beginning and the end.

In a standing posture, take a few silent breaths to prepare.

Breathe in through your mouth to the slow mental count of four. In your throat, make a breathy "aaaaah" sound as you inhale.

Do not use your vocal cords. Whisper the "aaaaah" sound with your throat.

Pause for a second with your lungs filled, then exhale while counting slowly to four in your mind. As you exhale through your mouth, round your lips and make an "oooooh" sound in your mouth. Again, whisper it—do not use your vocal cords. Pause for a second with your lungs empty.

Repeat this cycle a dozen times or so. Your lips will be more open as you make the "aaaaah" sound on the inhalation, and your lips will be rounded when you make the "oooooh" sound on the exhalation. Keep your throat open the whole time so that the breathy vowel sounds resonate within your chest.

End by taking a few silent breaths as you relax.

Exercise 2.7: Vowel Breathing

Adopt a standing posture and focus your gaze on the distant, unseen horizon that lies beyond the walls of your practice room. Take a few silent breaths to calm your thoughts and focus on what you are about to do.

Draw a deep breath through your nose. Exhale slowly with a sustained A vowel sound using your vocal cords. Keep your throat and mouth open so that the sound reverberates inside your body. Feel its vibrations. Do not try to stretch the sound out too long, but keep it even in tone and volume.

Aaaaaaaaaaaaaaaaay.

Draw a deep breath. Exhale with a sustained E vowel sound.

Eeeeeeeeeeeeeeeeeey.

Drawing a deep breath and exhale with a sustained I vowel sound.

Iiiiiiiiiiiiiiiiiiiiiiiiy.

Draw a deep breath and exhale with a sustained O vowel sound.

Ooooooooooooooh.

Draw a deep breath and exhale with a sustained U vowel sound.

Yuuuuuuuuuuuuuh.

Still your breath for three beats with your lungs empty. Repeat the sequence of vowel breaths four times.

Take a few slow, silent breaths to relax and end the exercise.

There must be no strain. When you inhale, do not completely fill your lungs, and when you sound the vowel sounds, do not completely empty them. Avoid trying to sustain the vowel sounds for too long. The work will charge you with energy and may make you feel a bit light-headed. If you find yourself coughing in a persistent way, you must stop the exercise and not try again for a few days.

Exercise 2.8: Working the Bellows

This exercise takes its name from the leather bellows blacksmiths once used to blow air into their fires, so that they could heat the iron they shaped with hammers on their anvils. It is a vigorous and healthful massage of your internal organs, and it cleanses and oxygenates the blood. It also raises occult energy within your body, which you will begin to feel after a few cycles of breath.

This exercise should be done in a sitting posture. Sit forward at the end of a wooden chair with your feet flat on the floor separated by about twelve inches and your hands on your knees.

Lean forward at an angle with your back straight and spread your elbows to the sides. Keep the top of your head in line with your spine. This will cause your face to be turned downward at a slight angle.

Begin to huff air into and out of your lungs in short, deep huffs through your open mouth, so that it makes an audible sound that is like panting. Drive the air in and out seven times in a rhythmic way that causes your diaphragm to bounce up and down and your abdomen to move in and out.

Pause at the end of this sevenfold cycle and sit upright. Take a single long, silent breath, inhaling and exhaling through your nose.

Lean forward and repeat this audible huffing in and out seven times. Sit up and take a long silent breath to relax. Repeat this sevenfold cycle four times at the beginning of your practice. When you become more experienced, you can extend the exercise to five, six, or seven cycles.

It is possible to do this exercise standing bent over, with the hands on the knees, but there is a danger of falling if you become dizzy, so it is safer to perform it sitting on the edge of a chair until you become accustomed to it.

To conclude the exercise, sit upright in the chair and take several slow, silent breaths.

Exercise 2.9: Death Breathing

The goal of this exercise is to quiet your mind and body as much as is possible in a waking state while sitting upright. Your chest should not rise or fall to any noticeable degree, so that anyone looking at you would not know you were still alive—hence the name of the exercise.

Adopt a sitting posture with your back straight, feet flat on the floor and twelve inches apart, and hands resting on the knees. Take a few silent breaths to focus on what you are about to do. Close your eyes and relax your body.

Begin to breathe more slowly. Breathe through your nose. Try to stir the air as little as possible. At the same time, make your breaths shallower, so that less air is passing in and out of your body.

Be aware of the air moving in and out through your nose. Be aware of the slight rise and fall of your chest. Be aware of your heartbeat, and make a deliberate effort of will to slow your heart rate.

Without causing undue strain, reduce as much as you are able the amount of air passing in and out of your body and the rate of your breaths. If you find yourself struggling to maintain the rhythm of your breaths, you are doing too much and should increase the amount of air you are breathing or the rate of your breaths to regain your composure.

It is better not to count your breaths, because this will distract your mind. Continue the exercise for about three to five minutes. If it is causing you strain, shorten this time; if you find it easy, lengthen the time, or better still, slow the tempo of your breaths.

To conclude, open your eyes and take a few deep, silent breaths.

Exercise 2.10: Dragon Breaths

This exercise will awaken the dragon fire of kundalini energy that lies sleeping within the root-center of your body, at the base of your spine. It will also strengthen your ability to manipulate occult energies. It can be quite strenuous—how much so depends entirely on how strenuous you are willing and able to make it. The goal is to produce perspiration on the surface of your skin and induce what is known in yoga as pore breathing. Again, let me stress the importance of not over-straining your lungs by trying to breathe too deeply in or out.

Adopt the sitting posture and take a few slow, silent breaths to focus your mind on what you are about to do.

Breathe in through your nose slowly and deeply without making a sound. If you cannot breathe through your nose, part your lips and breathe silently through your mouth. As you do so, lift your shoulders very slightly with your hand still resting on your knees to expand your chest. The inhalation must be slow, even, and controlled. In the beginning of your practice, try for around four or five seconds in duration. Count slowly and silently to yourself as you inhale.

Stop your breath without locking your throat and hold it for the same number of beats that you inhaled. If you inhale for five seconds, hold your lungs full for five seconds as you count them off slowly in your mind.

Relax your shoulders and exhale silently through your nose, or mouth if you cannot breathe through your nose, for the same number of seconds until your lungs are almost empty. Keep the outflow of your breath perfectly even. Take care not to allow your diaphragm to spasm in an uncontrolled way.

Hold your lungs empty for the same count. Again, do not lock your throat. Do not strain your abdominal muscles—keep your abdomen relaxed. Avoid tensing the muscles in your back, neck, arms, and legs. This is the most strenuous part of the four-fold cycle of breath. When you become aware that you are tensing your muscles, deliberately relax them and continue.

Repeat the four-fold cycle a dozen times or so, or until you feel a cooling perspiration on your skin. If the perspiration does not come in the first week or two of regular work, do not worry. It will occur with sufficient practice. To generate this perspiration, you must be able to control your urge to gasp for breath.

If you find yourself gasping air in an uncontrolled way, or if you find your diaphragm jerking with the effort to breathe, you are trying to do too much, too soon. Reduce the duration of your inhalations, exhalations, retentions, and exclusions, while still keeping them the same length. Instead of counting five on each part of the cycle, count four or three. With practice, you will find that you can increase the duration of your retentions and exclusions and also the number of breath cycles. Eventually, you may wish to do two dozen or three dozen cycles. Do not count the number of cycles—it distracts the mind.

When you are ready to stop the exercise, relax your body and draw a few deep, silent breaths in the normal way.

MEDITATION

Meditation is generally assumed to be an esoteric practice of China, India, Tibet, and other Eastern nations, but it has also been used by mystics in the West for thousands of years. We have no explicit texts describing the meditation used by the Egyptians, Greeks, and Romans of the ancient world, but it cannot be doubted that they used techniques to still and control their mental processes. Christian monks practiced a form of meditation throughout the Middle Ages called contemplation, during which they examined in their minds their past actions or considered the meaning of sacred teachings.

The most ancient form of Christian contemplation of which we have a written account is called the *Lectio Divina*. It consists of four stages: *lectio*, *meditatio*, *oratio*, and *contemplatio*. *Lectio*, in which a sacred verse of Scripture is read, is followed by *meditatio*, during which the meaning of the verse is silently considered. The response in the mind to meditation on the sacred verse leads to the third stage, *oratio*, in which a spontaneous prayer is uttered that is based on the comprehension of the verse during meditation. The final stage, *contemplatio*, consists in an inner appreciation of the spiritual enlightenment the first three steps have engendered.

In general, meditation may be described as the practice of sitting quietly and being aware of what is going on in your mind and body. You can meditate on many different things and in many different ways—on your state of being, your health, your past, your intentions, a particular idea, an image, a phrase or word, God, oneness, or nothingness.

At root, the purpose of all forms of meditation is to stop the flow of superficial chatter that is constantly running through your mind. Meditation techniques are designed to interrupt that chatter, if only for the limited period of time during which you meditate. When you break the stream of memories, emotions, words, and urges that runs through your head, you create a stillness in which transcendental insights can arise.

These insights are communications from an intelligence that is higher than your common consciousness. They may come from higher spirits, your higher self, your guardian angel, or deities. They usually pertain to moral, esoteric, or spiritual matters. It is during meditation that higher spirits can teach you a personal system of magic by directing your mind to needed areas of study and by suggesting new and unique ritual techniques.

As magicians, we ordinarily don't seek emptiness as a goal when we meditate. That is the goal of the mystic, who wants to escape from causal reality. Magicians seek to control and command reality, which is the environment in which magic is worked.

Meditation is useful in magic as a way of stilling the mind after a ritual procedure. Thoughts and desires running through the mind of a magician interfere with the realization of an act of magic that has just been worked. It is necessary to learn how to concentrate powerfully during the dramatization of the ritual purpose, and then to immediately turn the mind off to enable that purpose to be realized.

This requires a control over the thought process that is beyond the average person, who has never attempted to still the inner thought stream. It can only be achieved through the regular practice of harnessing the thoughts and stilling the mind, which is why exercises in meditation are so important.

TEN FORMS OF MEDITATION

I will list some of the common forms of meditation that are used by yogis in India and Buddhist monks in Tibet. They are all designed to control the thoughts so that thoughts cease to be the master and become the servant.

1. Thought Stream: The attention is turned inward to sustain an awareness of the stream of thoughts that spontaneously arise and pass through the mind.
2. Breath Awareness: The attention is focused on the sensations of breathing in and out.
3. Memory Review: The events of the day prior to the meditation period are remembered in their correct order and in as much detail as possible.
4. Instruction: A moral or esoteric teaching is considered in an effort to fully understand its higher meaning.
5. Emotion: A single emotion, such as love or pity, is held in the mind and considered in all its aspects.
6. Point Awareness: The attention is focused on a single point and held there like a fly pinned to the wall.
7. Mantra: A word or phrase is chanted over and over with full attention on the word or phrase.

8. Mandala: The mind is focused on an esoteric pattern, such as the *shri yantra*, in an effort to fully comprehend its significance.
9. Mudra: The thoughts are kept fixed on the position of the hands.
10. Empty Mind: The mind is held empty.

In the following exercises, you will learn how to still your thoughts and emotions in order to achieve an inner tranquility; how to turn away from desire for a result, which is fatal to the success of a ritual working; how to attain a mental state suitable for projecting your prayers and incantations; and how to open your mind to communications from higher spiritual intelligences who seek to instruct and guide you in your progress as a magician.

EXERCISES FOR CHAPTER 3

Exercise 3.1: Stepped Relaxation

This exercise, or something like it, is taught in almost every yoga instruction course, and it is also used in Western magic. I've even run across it in books dealing with self-hypnosis. It involves the progressive relaxation of the body in distinct stages, and it teaches how to first focus the attention on different parts of the body and then to withdraw that attention completely from those parts. In a general sense, it is a meditation on the body.

Take off your shoes. If you are wearing a wristwatch, take it off and set it aside. If you are wearing a belt or tie, make sure they are not too tight or remove them. It is important to avoid any clothing or jewelry that is constricting.

Lie on your back on the floor. If you wish, you may put a pillow or cushion under your head and cover yourself with a blanket to avoid becoming chilled. I always do this exercise with no pillow and no blanket, but then, cold has never bothered me.

Allow your feet to droop naturally out to the sides. Your heels should be around six inches apart. Stretch your arms down beside your body with your palms opened upward, and keep them far enough away from your hips that they do not touch.

Close your eyes. Take regular silent breaths and be aware of the places where your body presses against the floor. Take note of any tightness in any part of your body and consciously relax it.

Turn your awareness to your feet. Focus only on your feet. Curl your toes down and tighten the muscles in your feet. Hold them tight for a full cycle of silent breath, a slow inhalation and exhalation, then relax your feet completely.

Withdraw your attention from your feet, just as though they were no longer a part of your body. Focus on your calves and shins. Tighten the muscles in your lower legs and hold them tight for a cycle of silent breath, then relax them and withdraw your mind from them.

Turn your attention to your thighs. Tighten the muscles all around the upper part of your legs and hold them tight for a cycle of breath, then release them.

Focus on your buttocks. Tighten the muscles against the floor, hold them tight for a cycle of breath, then relax.

Turn your attention to your abdomen. Tighten your stomach muscles, hold them for a cycle of breath, and relax them completely.

Arch your lower back slightly as you tighten your back muscles. Hold them tight and be aware of them for a cycle of breath, then relax.

Shift your attention to your hands and arms. Clench your fists and tighten the muscles in your arms, hold them tight for a cycle of breath, then open your hands and relax them.

Tighten the muscles in your chest and shoulders, hold them tight for a cycle of breath, and relax.

Tighten your neck and throat, but keep your throat open so that you can breathe. Hold them tight for a cycle of breath, and relax.

Tighten the muscles of your face. Purse your lips and press them together, clench your jaw, frown, and squeeze your shut eyelids tight. Hold this scrunched-up expression for a cycle of breath, then relax.

Shift your awareness to the skin covering the top of your skull and hold it there. You have detached your consciousness from the rest of your body. Only be aware of a small circle in the center of the crown of your head. You float, bodiless, on a sea of velvet darkness. Continue to breathe silent breaths. If your attention wanders to any other part of your body, gently guide it away and back to the crown of your head.

Hold the focus of your awareness on the top of your head for several minutes, breathing regular silent breaths, then open your eyes to end the exercise.

Exercise 3.2: Auditing

If you are going to become a magician, you must become aware of what is going on inside your mind. You cannot control it unless you are aware of it. Usually, we allow the chaos in our minds to pass unnoticed, but it is possible to deliberately turn our attention upon it and observe it from a detached perspective, as though watching the thoughts of another person.

Sit in a chair in a quiet room with the light dimmed. I recommend that you use a plain kitchen chair without arms and adopt the sitting posture with your feet flat on the floor and about twelve inches apart, your back straight and leaning slightly forward, and your hands resting on your knees. However, if you find this posture uncomfortable, you can use a padded armchair.

Gaze straight forward at the unseen distant horizon, as though looking through the wall of the room, and take a couple of silent breaths to calm and focus. Close your eyes.

Turn your awareness to your own thoughts. Simply be conscious of what you are thinking. Hold your attention inward while continuing to breathe slow, silent breaths.

When you first try to do this, your mind will shut down, and you will only be conscious of yourself waiting for thoughts to arise. The only thought that will come will be "When are the thoughts going to come?" But the human mind is wayward and restless. It does not like to remain focused on one thing for long.

At some point, you will realize that your attention has drifted and that you have been thinking about something else. It may be something trivial. It doesn't matter what the thought was; be aware of it and take mental note of it. Of course, this will stop your thoughts once again, but if you wait patiently, again your attention will drift and other thoughts will arise.

It's important not to try to control the thoughts that come into your mind. For this exercise, it does not matter what those thoughts are. It only matters that you are aware of them as they arise and aware of what other thoughts they in turn give rise to. Allow yourself to think. Do not force it, but allow it to happen and observe it. Watch the way your mind works.

Continue in this way for around ten minutes, then open your eyes to end the exercise.

Exercise 3.3: Breath Awareness

This is an ancient yoga meditation that is both easy and difficult. It is easy to begin but difficult to sustain for any length of time, at least at the start of your practice.

In a quiet room with the lighting dimmed, assume the sitting posture that has already been described. Take a couple of silent breaths to prepare, and close your eyes.

Turn your attention to your breathing as you continue to take slow, silent breaths. Be aware of the rise and fall of your chest, the movements of your diaphragm. Be conscious of the air as it passes in and out through your nostrils. If you cannot breathe through your nose for some reason, breathe silently through your parted lips.

Try not to allow yourself to be distracted by other sensations in your body. If you notice that your attention has shifted to a tense muscle or to the noises your stomach is making, gently turn it back to your breathing.

Your mind will want to wander to other matters. Thoughts will arise in your head, and you will suddenly realize that your awareness has shifted from your breathing to your thinking. Gently guide your consciousness back to your breathing.

It is important to be gentle and not to become discouraged by the waywardness of your own mind. Only when you begin exercises in meditation do you truly realize how fickle, chaotic, and undisciplined your own mind is. We never really notice this chaos until we make the attempt to control it, and that is a humbling experience, because the mind does not want to be controlled.

Treat your mind like a willful, spoiled child, and discipline it with love and attention. It will gradually become better behaved. But if you are too harsh, it will rebel against your control.

Continue to be aware of your own breathing for around ten minutes. Do not time the exercise. The exact duration is unimportant. When you feel that around ten minutes have passed, open your eyes to end the exercise.

Exercise 3.4: Omega Mantra

A mantra is a word or phrase that is chanted over and over. It has a variety of uses. When passed from teacher to student, it can awaken insights or occult abilities. It can be used to trigger magic effects. Chanting a mantra in a mindful way induces an altered state of consciousness that invites spiritual or esoteric insights.

In this exercise, we will use what I refer to as the Omega mantra. Omega is the final letter of the Greek alphabet. It symbolically signifies totality and completion. The shape of the Greek letter is like the Latin letter O with its bottom opened. It resembles the open womb, ready either to receive a seed or to birth forth a child.

Assume the sitting posture in a quiet, dimly lit room and take a few silent breaths to relax and prepare.

Draw a normal breath and vocalize the word *Omega* in three syllables, extending each syllable on its vowel sound.

Ooooooh ... maaaaaay ... gaaaaaaah.

Take another normal breath and repeat the mantra, stretching it out so that it spans most of the exhalation.

Note that the vowel O, which is female in shape, comes at the beginning; the vowel A, which is male in shape, comes at the end; and the "may" sound between them represents you as you chant the mantra. In some parts of the English-speaking world, the word omega is pronounced "oh-mee-gah." This form can be used for the chant, if it is preferred. You unite the A and the O vowels, the Alpha and the Omega, the beginning and the end, in this chant.

It is not necessary for the purposes of this exercise to vocalize the mantra loudly. If you need to do it quietly, for reasons of privacy, you can sub-vocalize it by forming it with a whisper in your throat.

As you sound out the three parts of the mantra, be completely focused on the sounds you are making. Turn your mind to the sound of the mantra and do not permit it to wander. When you inhale between each vocalization of the mantra, focus on your breath. Breathe in through your nose and close your mouth as you inhale.

You will need to find a rhythm that you can sustain, one that will not leave you breathless. Continue chanting the mantra for several minutes with complete mindfulness of the sounds.

To end the exercise, take several slow, silent breaths and open your eyes.

Exercise 3.5: Mandala

A mandala is a sacred diagram that is meditated upon to achieve spiritual insights or magic abilities. Mandalas have been used extensively in Tibetan Buddhism and in Hindu tantra. They appear in Christianity in the form of the maze meditation, during which a devout Christian walks along the convoluted lines of a maze that is designed into a floor while reciting holy verses.

However, it is not necessary to actually walk the mandala, as the medieval Christians did—it is possible to project your consciousness inside the mandala merely by looking at its image.

Classical mandalas tend to have a central point as their focus, surrounded by a circle, which in turn is surrounded by a square. There are many variations, but this is the general pattern.

The most celebrated mandala is the *shri yantra*, a design with a central dot at the middle of a series of overlapping triangles, which are inside concentric circles, which in their turn are enclosed in a convoluted, four-sided box.

You can draw your own mandala for this exercise, and it does not need to be so complex as the *shri yantra*. As a practical matter, it is best to sketch the lines in with a very light touch of a pencil until you are sure you have the correct shapes, before making them heavy and permanent.

On a blank sheet of paper, put a dot in the center with your pencil. Draw an upright triangle around the dot that has sides of equal length. Make it about three inches long on each side. Enclose this upright triangle in an inverted triangle so that the smaller upright triangle touches the sides of the larger inverted triangle at its points. Draw a circle around the inverted triangle so that the points of the inverted triangle touch the circle. Draw a square around the circle so that the circle touches the four sides of the square.

When you've lightly sketched this mandala out in pencil and have it looking the way you want it, you can use a felt-tipped marker to trace in the central point and the geometric figures surrounding it with thick, black lines.

This mandala may appear simple, but it is quite potent for awakening occult perception. To use it, place it upright where you can see it, and adopt the sitting posture before it. Gaze at the central dot. Keep your eyes and your attention fixed on the dot. It is not necessary to strain your eyes—if you find yourself straining to look at the mandala, blink and relax your eyes for a few seconds. Your eyes are only an aid in focusing your awareness on the center of the mandala.

Hold your gaze and your attention on the central dot of the figure for around ten minutes while breathing slow, silent breaths. Be aware of any thoughts or insights that may arise in your mind during this time. Do not be surprised or alarmed if during the exercise you hear odd sounds, see movement or flashes of light, or feel soft touches on your skin. Remember, by performing these exercises, you are rewiring your brain and making yourself sensitive to things you could not previously sense.

To end the exercise, close your eyes for a short while to relax them, and rise from your chair.

Exercise 3.6: Mudra

A mudra is a hand position with esoteric or spiritual significance. Mudras can be used as the focus for fruitful meditations and have been used in this way by Christians, Hindus, and Buddhists for many centuries. Even Islam uses hand gestures during ritual worship.

Sit before a table or desk in your practice room. The lighting should be dimmed. Take a couple of silent breaths to still your thoughts and focus on what you are about to do.

There are many possible mudras. In this exercise, I will teach you one that I use myself quite often.

Fold the fingers of your two hands together with the tips of your thumbs touching. Spread your index fingers so that the tips touch. While holding your hands still interlocked, extend your little fingers and touch the tips together. Keep your middle and ring fingers folded down over the backs of your knuckles to press your hand together.

Rest your elbows on the surface of your table or desk, and lean slightly forward so that you can press the joined tips of your thumbs against the point where the bridge of your nose meets your forehead. Your index fingers will point straight upward.

Experiment with your sitting position so that you can assume this posture without strain and can hold it for an extended period.

While in this position, close your eyes and be aware of the darkness of your closed eyelids. Breathe silent breaths. Maintain this pose for around ten minutes. Take mental note of any image that arises against the backdrop of your closed eyelids.

To end the exercise, open your eyes, sit back, and unlace your hands.

If you wish, you can combine this mudra with the Omega mantra and chant the mantra while holding the mudra pose.

Exercise 3.7: Body Awareness

It is important that you have quiet and not be interrupted for the duration of the exercise. Dim the lights or draw shut the curtains to produce a twilight effect in your practice room.

Adopt the sitting posture on a kitchen chair, or if you wish, sit in a comfortable armchair. Take a few slow, silent breaths to relax and focus your mind on what you are about to do. Close your eyes.

Be aware of the harmony and balance within your mind and body. Feel your own regular heartbeats. Become aware of the slight ringing in your ears that is always present but that we usually ignore and do not hear. Be aware of the balance of your muscles as they pull against each other to maintain the shape of your body. Feel the surface of your skin. Feel your own inner heat.

As you hold a collective awareness of your entire body in your mind, be conscious that you are separate and apart from your body. You are the observer, observing something apart from your own identity, your own true self. We can only observe something when we are separate from it. Usually we consider our body a part of us, but the true self is not the body.

Observe the perfect balance and harmony of your body in all its parts as something outside yourself, as though it were the body of a stranger. Observe it passively, without causing any part of it to change or move. Continue in this body awareness for ten minutes or so.

To end, open your eyes and take a few slow, silent breaths.

Exercise 3.8: Contemplation

The name of this exercise refers to the modern definition of contemplation, the practice of thinking deeply about something.

Sit in the sitting posture in a quiet, dimly lit room and breathe deeply and silently a few times to calm and focus your mind. Close your eyes.

In this exercise, you will think about all aspects of a single abstract concept or principle, keeping your mind trained on it to the exclusion of all other thoughts. A few examples of abstract concepts that work well for the purpose are truth, justice, honor, loyalty, beauty, goodness, mercy, forgiveness, hope, love, and charity.

It is best to avoid contemplation of hurtful or hateful concepts. Practice only with principles that are positive and life-affirming.

Choose one from the list I have given and consider it. First ask yourself what it means, and then ask what it means to you on a personal level. Think about examples of it that you have observed in yourself and in family members. Consider the effects and consequences of its application, how it changes the lives and attitudes of those with whom it interacts. Ask yourself what is best about it.

Continue in this way, examining the principle from all sides in your mind, asking yourself questions and drawing conclusions, for ten or fifteen minutes. Do not time the exercise. Just estimate when this period has passed, or stop when your mind becomes tired and begins to wander.

Open your eyes and draw a few silent breaths to end the exercise.

Exercise 3.9: Prayer

One of the most important forms of meditation is prayer. In Western magic, prayer is used extensively to communicate with the higher self, the personal guardian angel, the other angels, and the gods, including your highest concept of God, whether that be Jesus Christ, God the Father, the Queen of Heaven, the Virgin Mary, the Buddha, Vishnu, or another form of the creative principle.

Articulate prayer, whether it is spoken aloud or only voiced silently in the mind, is a form of incantation and will be examined in chapter 7, but in this exercise, we will practice achieving the most useful state of mind for making prayer an effective instrument in your occult work.

The most important thing to understand about prayer is that it is active. When you pray in any form, you are sending out a message that you want some other intelligence to receive, comprehend, and respond to. This is true even in religious prayers of adoration and praise, because when you adore a god, you are telling the god that you are devoted to that god and are in harmony with the god's nature and purpose.

There is really no such thing as a prayer made without expectation. All prayer is a dynamic interaction between the person who prays and the being to whom the prayer is directed.

In order to get the best result from a prayer, you must pray with clarity of intention using explicit words that cannot be misunderstood. Your prayer must concern only one topic. If it is convoluted, is vague, or concerns multiple topics, it will lack force and clarity. Keep your prayer simple and keep it unified.

Prayer has two phases. The first is a powerful sending out of the message of the prayer, and the second is a calm inner conviction that the prayer has been received. The projection phase lasts for the full duration of the actual words of the prayer. The calm assurance occurs immediately thereafter and is sustained in the back of the mind without doubt or questioning.

For this exercise, choose something you wish to request of an angel or deity whom you trust completely and know will never harm you in any way. As an example, you might choose the following brief prayer to the Queen of Heaven:

Goddess, bless this house and all who
dwell beneath its roof with good health.

This is only an example. You can make your prayer much longer than this, provided that it has a central focus of purpose that is clear and positive. It is a good idea to compose the prayer you will speak beforehand, so that you will not be fumbling for words during the actual speaking of it. Sometimes it can be effective to pray spontaneously, directly from the heart, but always with clarity and focus.

Adopt the sitting posture in a quiet, dimly lit room. Draw a few silent breaths to prepare your mind. Close your eyes.

Consider the deity or higher spirit to whom the prayer will be directed. Hold the spirit in your mind, not only an image of the spirit but the qualities you know of the spirit. Imagine that you are sitting with the spirit, that the spirit is only a short distance away watching and listening to you.

Speak the words of the prayer directly and sincerely while continuing to hold the spirit present in your mind. You do not need to speak out loud, but if you speak silently, you must articulate the words of your prayer in your mind so that you can hear them inwardly as clearly as though you had voiced them aloud.

Repetition is useful in prayer. Repeat the prayer over and over if it is brief. If you are praying spontaneously and composing the words as you go along, continue to pray in the same vein for several minutes while holding an intense awareness of the spirit to whom you are speaking. Be aware that this spirit is not distant but is right there with you, listening to you.

When you finish speaking the prayer, make your mind empty and tranquil. Allow the spirit to fade from your thoughts. Do not think about the spirit to whom the prayer was directed or about the content of the prayer. Do not wonder if it has been received. I can't stress this point strongly enough because it is absolutely vital to successful prayer. You must have no desire or expectation in your mind or heart after speaking the prayer. All the desire is projected during the speaking of it, and after you finish speaking it, there must be no desire or expectation about it.

Take a few silent breaths, open your eyes, and go about your day. If you find your mind creeping back to the prayer, wondering if it was received, if it will be answered, if it was worded correctly, you must clear your mind gently and firmly and turn it to some everyday task.

Exercise 3.10: Spiritual Guidance

When you begin to study practical magic, there are many spiritual beings who are eager to guide and teach you. They have always been there, but it is only when you turn your mind toward occult things that they come forward with their teachings. This process can be facilitated by meditating on openness of mind.

Sit as usual in the sitting posture and breathe a few silent breaths before beginning. Close your eyes.

Still your thoughts. Listen to the silence. If there are distracting sounds from elsewhere in the building, ignore them and listen to the silence that is within you. Hold this silence for several minutes. Speak these words, either out loud or silently in your mind:

> *My teachers, I open myself to you. Teach me what I must know of the art of magic. Guide your humble student in the ways of your wisdom.*

If you have a specific occult matter that you wish to learn about or gain insight into, modify this invitation to include the specific topic.

Make your mind tranquil, and when thoughts arise, observe them without emotion. Do not think about anything deliberately, but merely keep your mind quiet and receptive. When thoughts arise, merely observe them. You can consider your insights after the exercise is finished. Continue in this way for ten or fifteen minutes, or until your mind is tired.

Open your eyes and take a few silent breaths to end the exercise.

VISUALIZATION

One of the essential skills every magician must acquire in order to work magic successfully is *visualization*—a general term for sensory imagining, the forming of symbols, images, scenes, and other sense impressions such as sounds, touches, smells, or tastes in the imagination. Whenever you picture anything in your mind in a sensory way, you are using visualization. You can visualize something as simple as a geometric shape or as complex as a moving scene involving many people with conversations, odors, and physical contact.

The deaf and the blind are not excluded from visualization work. Most who are blind could see once and can remember seeing. Most who are deaf or hard of hearing can hear some sounds or were able to hear at one time and can imagine sounds. Those who have been blind from birth will not be able to use mental images but must rely mainly on sounds for visualization work, and those deaf from birth cannot use sounds but must rely mainly on images.

When performing any work of magic, we visualize the enactment and fulfillment of our purpose. This enactment usually takes a symbolic form. For example, suppose you worked a ritual to free a woman from her emotional bondage to an abusive husband. You might visualize her emotional dependence on the man as a set of chains binding her to a stone wall. You might then visualize those chains breaking and falling off her wrists and ankles, and the woman walking away from the wall and through the open door of her prison. The chains symbolize her bondage to her husband, the breaking of the chains her freedom, and her passage through the open door her departure from the marriage.

It is important that you practice visualization until you are able to see images in your imagination clearly and are able to sustain them for as long as you wish. You must also be able to create other sensory impressions in your mind, such as scents, sounds, and physical sensations. This requires work, but there is no gain without effort. Think of it as muscle building for the mind. The more you do it, the easier it becomes and the better you get at it.

LEARNING TO VISUALIZE

Learning to visualize is a bit like learning the game of chess. The rules of chess are simple. Anyone can learn them and be playing the game in a single evening. But to be good at chess takes years of practice, and some players are always going to be better than others due to their innate natural ability.

Practice visualizing simple objects. Sit down in a quiet place around the same time every day and spend ten or fifteen minutes forming these images in your mind. First look at the object, then close your eyes and imagine the object with as much clarity as you can manage. When the object becomes dim in your imagination, open your eyes for a few seconds and refresh its image in your mind, then close your eyes and visualize it. Do this with small things such as a pencil, a coffee mug, a book, a set of keys, a wristwatch, and so on.

After you gain some skill in holding simple static images in your mind, begin to practice visualizing the faces of other people you know, such as friends, family members, and coworkers. Play them in your mind as if you were watching a short video clip. When you get some practice at this, move on to more complex moving scenes, such as street traffic, people on a beach, children playing in a playground, an airplane taking off from a runway, and so on. Finally, add sounds to your visualization, such as people talking to each other, children laughing, dogs barking, or traffic noises.

Visualization involves other senses as well as sight. It's easier to visualize an image than a sound for most people, so it's a good idea to start with images. But don't neglect to practice visualizing sounds. These can be used to good effect in your rituals. For the strongest effect, include odors and sensations of touch in your visualizations. Think of visualization as a ritual instrument and practice learning how to use it, just as you would practice with a guitar to learn to play it.

The graded visualization exercises that follow should be practiced regularly for a period of at least six months. You don't need to practice them exclusively—you can do other exercises as well during the same period. The longer you continue these exercises, the better your ability to visualize will become. It is a vital part of magic, so you cannot do visualization exercises too often.

It is best to pick a certain time of day when you can do a visualization without being interrupted, a time when you are always able to withdraw into solitude for this practice. If you have no chance to get away from others, it is possible to do these exercises by simply closing your eyes and withdrawing your mind from outer distractions, even if you are in a crowded place, but it is easier to do them in a quiet place.

EXERCISES FOR CHAPTER 4

Exercise 4.1: Visualizing Static Objects

Sit down before a table or desk with a pencil lying on the surface in front of you. Keep your back straight and your hands on your knees, or rest them on the arms of your chair if you choose to use an armchair. Take a few slow, silent breaths to prepare your mind.

Look closely at the pencil without straining your eyes. Study all its details, then close your eyes and attempt to see the pencil in your mind, exactly as it was when you looked at it with your eyes. Visualize not only the shape of the pencil but also its colors and the shadow it casts on the table.

When you find yourself having difficulty holding the image in your mind, open your eyes for a few moments to refresh the image, then close them again and hold the image in your imagination. Each time your mind wanders or you begin to lose the mental image of the pencil, open your eyes briefly to look at it, then close them again.

Continue in this way for around ten minutes, or until your mind becomes fatigued. Do not try to do this exercise for longer than this. The best results come while your mind is fresh and alert.

To end the exercise, open your eyes and take a few slow, silent breaths.

You can do variations on this exercise using other simple objects that you can pick up with your hand. Try it with an apple, a flower, a teacup, a book, a quarter, a rock, a thimble, a rubber band. Just keep the objects small and simple. Do each object a few times, then move on to another simple object.

Exercise 4.2: Visualizing Mental Shapes

Sit down and take a few silent breaths to prepare. Close your eyes and picture in your mind a cube that is outlined in thin, straight segments of wire. Imagine it to be around four inches in size. Picture it floating in a black space, the silvery wire that makes up its edges the only thing you can see.

Do not strain to see the cube. If you find yourself compressing your eyelids or squinting, relax. Keep the muscles of your body relaxed as well. Remember, you are exercising your mind, not your eyes and not your body. It is easy to tense up as you focus your mind to concentrate on a visualization. All your energies should be applied to the mental level, not the physical.

When you can clearly see the wire frame of the cube, cause it to turn slowly so that you view it from other angles. Turn it back and forth, then fix it in each position for a few seconds while you contemplate its appearance.

Open your eyes and take a few silent breaths to end.

You can perform variations on this visualization of an imagined object, but keep the things you visualize very simple—a ball, a golf tee, a hammer, a brick, a comb. Ten minutes is long enough for this exercise, which you can do anywhere that is quiet enough to allow you to concentrate—but the best results will be achieved if you do this exercise at the same time of day and in the same location.

Exercise 4.3: Visualizing Moving Objects

Sit with your back straight, hands on your knees, feet twelve inches or so apart, and breathe deeply and silently through your nose a few times to focus your intention on the exercise you are about to do.

Close your eyes and picture in your mind a flag rippling gently in the breeze on top of a flagpole. See in your mind the motion of the flag and notice its colors. You may visualize any flag you wish, but it will be easier if you pick a flag design that you know well.

As a general rule, it is best if these visualization exercises are done sitting rather than lying down, as it allows the mind to remain more alert. You will find when you begin these exercises that your mind will play tricks on you to try to avoid the work. One such trick is to make you sleepy and cause your thoughts to wander.

Open your eyes and breathe slowly and deeply through your nose several times to clear your thoughts before going about your day.

Variations on this visualization of a moving object might include such things as a stream of water flowing out of a tap, a bumble bee buzzing around an open flower, a cloud moving across the sky, a white sheet drying in the breeze on a clothesline, or leaves falling from a tree.

Exercise 4.4: Visualizing Human Faces

Sit in the sitting posture and draw several silent breaths to prepare.

Close your eyes. Think of the face of someone you know, and imagine that person smiling and talking. Don't worry about what they are saying or about hearing the sound of their voice. Picture in your mind all the details of the person's face. It can be the face of a family member, a coworker, a neighbor, or even a celebrity you have seen on television, but it should be a face that you have seen often and know quite well.

Cause the face to turn this way and that. Take note of the eye color and hair color of the person, and visualize various expressions.

If you find that your mind is blocked and you can't recall the features of the person, which sometimes happens even with the faces of those we know very well, just choose another person's face to visualize. Do this for ten minutes or so.

Open your eyes and clear your mind with several silent breaths to end the exercise.

Exercise 4.5: Visualizing Places

Adopt the sitting posture and take a few silent breaths.

Close your eyes. Imagine a familiar place that you have stood in many times or a place near your home that you have often visited. It can even be a room in your own house. Visualize this location both in front of you and all around you. In your mind, turn your head this way and that to see things at your sides and even behind you. Do not move your physical head—all the movement is in your mind. Mentally walk around the place, looking at various features and objects.

Continue in this way for ten minutes or so, then open your eyes and draw a few silent breaths to end.

You can do this exercise with your own house, a summer house, a public space such as a library or schoolroom, a field, the bank of a river, a beach, the crest of a hill, a forest glade—any place you know well.

Exercise 4.6: Visualizing a Person Talking

In the sitting posture, draw a few slow, silent breaths to clear and focus your mind, and close your eyes.

See in your mind a person you know quite well sitting across from you in a room you are familiar with—your living room, for example. Visualize the entire person sitting before you. The person is talking to you. Imagine the sound of the person's voice, and imagine what the person is saying to you. Take note of the person's facial expressions and tone of voice as they speak to you. They will smile, move their hands, clear their throat, blink, turn their head. See everything about the person as clearly as possible, and hear the sound of their voice that you know so well.

Do this for ten minutes or so, then open your eyes and take a few silent breaths to clear your mind.

You can do this exercise using different people from both your present and past life, even those who have died. For example, you might choose to visualize your dead grandmother as you remember her from your childhood.

It is not important what the person is saying to you, only that you clearly remember in your mind the person's manner of speaking and the tone of their voice. It should echo in your head just as you remember it.

Exercise 4.7: Visualizing a Crowd

Sit comfortably in the sitting posture, take a few silent breaths, and close your eyes.

Imagine that you are at a party. The guests are mostly people you know. It may be a birthday party, a holiday event such as a Thanksgiving get-together, an office party where you work, or a housewarming—whichever form of social gathering you feel comfortable attending.

Walk through the rooms where the party is being held and interact with the people there, listening to them speak and speaking back to them in your imagination. Feel the brush of their clothing against you as they pass close, feel the glass you hold in your hand. Smell the scents of the food being served, the perfume on the women.

Try to actually hear in your mind the sounds of their voices and your own voice replying to them. Hear them laughing. Hear the general babble of voices in the background. There may be soft music playing, the tinkle of wine glasses, the clatter of silverware if you are seated at a dining table.

You can choose which people you wish to interact with in this visualization. Focus on those people but remain aware of the entire scene that surrounds you. You are not detached from this scene; you are actually standing or sitting within it as you visualize it.

Before your concentration begins to falter, open your eyes and draw several deep, silent breaths to relax and end the exercise.

Exercise 4.8: Visualizing an Unfamiliar Figure

Assume the sitting posture in a quiet room and take a few slow, silent breaths to relax.

Close your eyes. Imagine standing before you an angel with widespread, feathered wings on his back. He has golden hair and a handsome, gentle face. His wings are iridescent and flash with every color of the rainbow like the tail of a peacock as he moves them gently. He wears a white robe. Upon the breast of this robe is the symbol of a golden circle with a golden dot in its center. As you imagine him in your mind, he smiles directly at you and raises his right hand in a gesture of blessing.

The value of this exercise is the visualization of something you have never seen before. You create this three-dimensional, animated figure in your imagination. It is important that it be a figure you have not seen.

You can vary this exercise by imagining different human beings unknown to you, angels of different appearances, or creatures unknown to you, such as those from Greek mythology.

Do not visualize anything horrifying or frightening. Keep your figures nonthreatening. You do not wish emotion to interfere with your visualization, which is the purpose of the exercise.

At times, spiritual beings may choose these complex visualizations to appear before you and deliver messages to you. If this happens, accept the message and remember it, but try not to become emotionally engaged. All your energies must be directed into creating the figure with as much tangible reality as possible. Don't allow yourself to be easily sidetracked by the content of the visualization.

If a spirit appears in a persistent way and indicates that it has important information to convey to you, you may wish to make this part of your ritual work, but then it ceases to be a mere exercise in visualization and becomes a spirit working. Try to stay focused on the act of visualization, not on the things visualized.

Open your eyes and draw a few silent breaths to end.

Exercise 4.9: Visualizing Energy Flowing Through Your Body

Adopt the sitting posture and take a few silent breaths to focus on what you are about to do.

Close your eyes. Imagine a cooling energy on the top of your head, like cool water, and then visualize the sensation of it flowing down through the inside of your body to your feet. Hold the coolness inside yourself, allowing it to fill you up the way water fills a vessel; then allow the coolness to drain out through the soles of your feet and through the floor beneath you until you are entirely emptied of the sensation of coolness.

As a variation, feel warmth on the top of your head, and allow this warmth to flow into your body, filling successively your head, your shoulders, your arms and hands, your chest and heart, your stomach and bowels, your thighs and shins, and finally your feet. Hold this warmth within you for a minute or so, then allow it to flow down through the soles of your feet and through the floor beneath you.

Do not visualize this energy as discomforting. It should be a gentle and pleasant coolness or a gentle and pleasant warmth. You can picture this energy visually soaking down through your body if you wish, but the main focus of the exercise should be on the sensation the energy causes inside you. Try to feel it as a real sensation.

Another variation is to imagine electrical energy flowing from a place above your head, over the outside of your skin. It is like static electricity. You can feel it lift the little hairs at the back of your neck and on your arms and legs as it flows down your body to your feet. It is not an unpleasant feeling, but it is strange, like the sensation you get when the air around you is charged with lightning. Let this electrical energy flow down into the floor, gradually leaving the surface of your skin and returning you to a normal condition.

To end, open your eyes and draw several silent breaths.

Exercise 4.10: Visualizing Your Breath

Adopt the sitting posture and take a few silent breaths to focus your mind.

Close your eyes. Visualize the air around you as a cloud of sparkling golden particles, like dust motes shining in sunlight, almost too small to see. They dance around you in constant vibratory motion.

When you have a clear visualization of these tiny sparks of golden light, breathe in slowly and deeply through your nose, and as you do so, see the golden particles flow into your chest, filling your lungs. See your lungs glow with golden light inside your body so brightly that the light shines out through your chest. Hold your breath for a few moments, and visualize the golden particles circulating and spreading throughout your body from your chest along your legs and arms, even to the tips of your fingers and toes.

Release your breath slowly and evenly, and as you do so, visualize the air that issues from your nostrils as a cloud of tiny black particles. These surround your head and shoulders for a brief time, then disperse into the golden air and become invisible.

Turn your attention back to your body and see the golden light inside you, still glowing gently. Feel its warmth, and note how it energizes your muscles and banishes fatigue.

Repeat this cycle five times. First, see the golden flecks of light in the air around you. Then draw them into your lungs with a slow inhalation and see them inside your chest. Visualize them spreading throughout your body as you retain the breath. Then visualize the tiny black specks on the exhalation that is released through your nose dispersing into the golden glowing air around you and vanishing from sight.

Open your eyes and take a few silent breaths to clear your mind.

CHAPTER 5

CONCENTRATION

Concentration is the ability to focus your mind intensely on one thing, without wavering from it for prolonged periods of time. With focus comes power. The sun's rays will not normally start a fire by themselves, but if you concentrate them through a magnifying glass, they will ignite a fire. Concentration is like a magnifying glass—it focuses all the power of your will on a single point.

Essential to any successful work of magic is the ability to focus the attention strongly and to hold that focus without allowing it to drift. You must be able to concentrate your attention both on your purpose, which you hold in the back of your mind, and on the symbolic actions realizing the purpose, which you simultaneously visualize.

No one ever realizes how weak their concentration is until they try to maintain it for longer than a minute or two. The untrained person has almost no ability to sustain attention on one chosen thing for more than a very brief period. Other thoughts distract the mind, which soon becomes tired and bored. When you begin to practice concentration, only then will you understand just how weak your concentration is, but if you keep at it, your ability to concentrate your attention will quickly become stronger.

HOW TO PRACTICE CONCENTRATION

The general form of practice is quite simple—you hold your gaze and your attention on one thing without allowing your mind to leave it. There is no need to strain your eyes. You can blink whenever you feel like it. The important part of the exercise is to keep awareness on your target. Those who are blind should practice by using other senses, such as hearing and touch.

In the beginning, your attention will wander after only a few minutes. You will find yourself thinking of something else and realize that you have been daydreaming. When this happens, gently guide your awareness back to the focus and hold it there.

You can use the same objects to practice your concentration that you used to practice static visualization. Use whatever you happen to have lying around where you live. It doesn't matter what you concentrate on, only that you hold your attention without wavering. Try to work up to ten minutes or so. This may take a few weeks, or you may be able to achieve it on the first try. Be honest with yourself. If your mind wanders, be aware of it and guide it back. Training the mind is a bit like training a dog. You succeed with firmness, gentleness, and persistence.

Your mind is in constant interaction with nonphysical levels of reality, which in occult studies are sometimes known as the astral planes. Think of them as different frequencies of vibration, like different radio channels. They exist simultaneously all around you, but normally you remain unaware of them, and the inhabitants of these planes of reality ignore you.

When you concentrate your will, it is like sending up a signal flare through those astral planes. The beings that exist on those planes, which we call spirits, immediately take notice of you. Suddenly, you are active and present in their worlds. The power of concentration is essential if you wish these beings to interact with you in a productive way when you work magic.

Concentration is also necessary for the exercise of willpower. The power of the will is what allows you to manipulate esoteric energies. By willing these energies to flow where you wish them to go, you can channel and move them, but this is only possible if you are able to focus the power of your will with unwavering intensity and clarity. You need concentration to successfully work magic.

Below are some basis exercises that will strengthen your ability to concentrate your mind.

EXERCISES FOR CHAPTER 5

Exercise 5.1: Concentration on a Stone

The purpose of this exercise is to train your mind to focus for extended periods on a simple object.

Find a small stone at the beach or on the side of the road. It doesn't matter where you find it, but pick up a stone that has some interesting feature that attracts your attention. It may be an odd shape or an unusual color or have contrasting inclusions within the stone that give it an interesting pattern.

Go to a place that is quiet where you will not be interrupted, and remove anything from your field of vision that is distracting. The lighting in the room should be soft and indirect.

Assume the sitting posture with the stone in front of you on a desk or table. Take a few silent breaths to relax and calm your mind. Look intently at the stone, but do not strain your eyes. All the intensity should be in your mind—your body must remain relaxed. If you feel yourself tensing up or feel your eyes straining, deliberately relax the tenseness while keeping your attention on the stone.

Examine every detail of the stone that is visible to you, holding your gaze without wavering on it. At the same time, hold your mind on it. Try to be aware of every tiny irregularity in its surface.

After you have held your concentration on the stone for three to five minutes, expand your awareness of it to the side you cannot see, and remember every detail of the hidden side of the stone that you saw when you previously examined it. Try to see the side of the stone that is in front of you and the side that is turned away from you at the same time in your mind. Do this for another few minutes.

Do not time the exercise. Estimate in your mind when you have been concentrating for ten minutes. The exact duration is of no importance. What matters is how steadily you can sustain your focus on the stone.

You will discover that your mind resents your effort to force it to concentrate. It will quickly try to wander, and the more tired you become, the more easily it will wander. You will find yourself thinking of other things without even being aware of how the thoughts crept into your mind. When this happens, gently turn your focus away from the intruding thoughts and bring your attention back to the stone.

End the exercise with a few slow, silent breaths as you relax your mind.

Exercise 5.2: Concentration on a Candle Flame

Place a small holder for a single candle on your desk or table and put a plain white candle in it. Utility candles of the kind you buy for when the electricity goes out work best. If you don't own a candle holder, you can melt the bottom of the candle and stick it to the center of a saucer or small plate.

Do not do this exercise in total darkness. The light from the candle will strain your eyes and make you see spots. Do it in a softly illuminated room. The source of the room light, whether it is a window or a lamp, should be behind you or to the side, not in front of you where it will be a distraction.

Light the candle on a table, sit comfortably in the sitting posture, and take a few silent breaths to calm your thoughts. When you are ready, look at the flame. Your mind must be wholly focused on the flame itself, but do not strain your eyes. When you notice your muscles tensing up around your eyes or in any other part of your body, consciously relax them without moving or taking your eyes off the flame.

The point of the exercise is to not daydream and to not think of other things. You must think only of the flame that you are gazing at, but you must think about it without words. Blink your eyes whenever you need to; there is no need to stare. The intensity of your focus must be mental, not in your eyes or any other part of your body.

Try to sustain this focus for around ten minutes. It is a lot harder than you might think. When you realize that your thoughts have wandered—and they will—bring your awareness gently back to the flame and hold it there.

When you feel yourself becoming mentally exhausted, close your eyes and take a few slow, silent breaths.

Exercise 5.3: Projection of Self into a Candle Flame

Light a plain white candle in its holder on your table or desk and sit in front of it. Take care that you are far enough away that your soft, regular exhalations do not disturb the flame in any way. Draw a few silent breaths to still your thoughts.

Gaze with full concentration at the flame for several minutes, holding only the flame in your awareness. Now imagine yourself reduced in size and standing inside the flame, surrounded by the flame but unburned by it. The flame cannot hurt you in any way. Imagine the flame to be like an aura around your body.

You must simultaneously gaze at the flame from your chair and place yourself standing inside the flame. This doublethink requires practice. It is not something we do in our daily lives. You must maintain full concentration on the flame, as you see it from your chair, and yet be completely aware of standing inside the flame that surrounds your standing body like an aura.

Hold this dual awareness in your mind for around five minutes, then relax your concentration, close your eyes, and take a few slow, silent breaths.

Exercise 5.4: Lengthening a Candle Flame

The room should be softly illuminated to prevent eyestrain. Light a white candle in a holder on the desk or table in front of you. Assume the sitting posture in your chair and calm your thoughts with a few silent breaths.

Gaze at the candle flame with full concentration for several minutes, focusing all your awareness only on the flame. As you continue to look at it, use the power of your will to lengthen the flame of the candle. Project the force of your will into the flame and pull the flame upward from the wick. A good way to do this is to imagine that you are the flame and to lengthen your flame-body by stretching it upward.

The flame will rise and fall as your concentration strengthens or weakens. Again, it is important that you do not strain your eyes or your muscles. Avoid glaring at the candle. Avoid clenching your jaw. Be aware from time to time of the muscles in your abdomen and neck, and if you feel them tensing up, deliberately relax them. Be aware of your thigh muscles and relax them if they become tense. Willpower is not in your body; it is in your mind.

You will discover that you can lengthen the flame to extraordinary lengths with this exercise, sometimes up to a foot above the wick depending on the type of candle you use. Continue in this way for ten minutes or so. Stop when you feel yourself becoming tired. The value in this exercise comes from brief, regular daily repetitions, not from forcing yourself to continue when you are weary.

As usual, you should close your eyes and take several silent breaths to relax your mind and end the exercise.

Exercise 5.5: Concentration on Incense Smoke

The room should be softly illuminated. It makes no difference which kind of incense you use for this exercise—pick one that you find pleasant. Put a stick of incense in a holder on your desk or table, light it, and sit in the sitting posture. Close your eyes and take a few silent breaths to calm your thoughts.

Open your eyes and direct all your attention to the rising column of smoke a few inches above the incense stick. Be aware of the way the smoke ripples and twists. Keep your mind wholly focused on the smoke and empty of all words or images.

For this exercise, make sure you are far enough away from the incense stick that your breaths do not disturb the column of smoke, and avoid moving in a way that creates eddies in the air of the room.

After ten minutes or so, or when you become tired and start to lose concentration, close your eyes and relax your mind as you take a few slow, silent breaths to end the exercise.

Exercise 5.6: Concentration on a Ticking Clock

You can improve your ability to concentrate by using your ears as well as your eyes. Find a clock that has a loud ticking and place it where you can sit next to it. Adopt the sitting posture and close your eyes. Take a few deep, silent breaths.

Without opening your eyes, focus your attention on the ticks of the clock and on nothing else. Don't think of anything. Don't pay attention to other sounds. Listen to the ticking with sustained concentration for around ten minutes.

You will know when your concentration wanders—you will suddenly realize you have not been hearing the ticking of the clock because your mind was elsewhere. This is normal for an undisciplined mind. Just bring your attention gently back to the sound of the ticking. Never become angry with yourself. Each time your thoughts wander and you realize it, guide your mind gently but firmly back to the ticking of the clock.

As a variation, you can do this exercise with a metronome, which is a device used by music students to keep perfect time when playing music. Any regular sound will serve as a focus, such as a foghorn or the sound of waves breaking on a beach. Music is not good for this exercise, however. It is not regular enough.

Take a few silent breaths and open your eyes to end the exercise.

Exercise 5.7: Clock Watching

There is another exercise you can do with a clock or watch. Take up the sitting posture in front of a table and close your eyes as you calm your restless mind with a few slow, silent breaths.

Look at the minute hand of the clock or watch on the table. Keep your attention on the minute hand without looking away from it as it moves imperceptibly on the clock dial. Do this without losing focus for five minutes or so.

Remember not to strain your eyes or to tense any other muscles in your body. When you become aware that some part of your body has tensed up, relax it as you continue with the exercise.

It is best to use a clock with a large dial for this study in concentration. A clock without a second hand is to be preferred, because the movement of the second hand is a distraction for the eyes. But if you have nothing else, you can do this exercise with an ordinary wristwatch.

When you decide to end the exercise, close your eyes and take a few silent breaths.

Exercise 5.8: Concentration on the Tetragram

This exercise requires both visualization and concentration. On a piece of paper, draw a square so that one of the corners of this square points upward, from your perspective, giving it a diamond shape. Put two crossing lines through the center of the square that run from its corners. This figure is what I call a tetragram. We will use it here as a focus for concentration exercises.

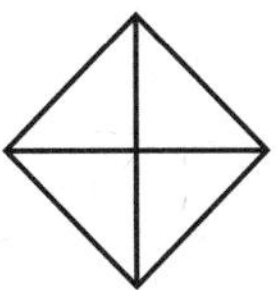

Sit in your chair in the sitting posture and take a few slow, silent breaths to relax and prepare your mind. Gaze at the tetragram, holding it in your mind with full concentration. Allow no other thoughts to intrude. Your mind should contain only the image of the tetragram. Do not even concentrate on the page it is drawn on, but hold just the figure itself in your thoughts. Be aware of its corners, its angles, and its center point that is defined by the lines that cross through its center. Do this for several minutes, and when your mind wanders, draw it gently back to the tetragram.

Close your eyes, but continue to hold the tetragram in your mind. You can picture it as black lines on a white background or as white lines on a black background, whichever seems easier. In fact, it is useful to mentally change the colors of the lines and the background from time to time, seeing the image of the tetragram for a minute or so as black lines on white, and then for another minute as white lines on black, alternating back and forth several times.

In your mind, trace the outer square of this figure clockwise, starting with the uppermost point of the diamond, then do the same thing in a counterclockwise direction. Mentally do this slow circling around the figure from each of its remaining three points, first clockwise, then counterclockwise. Then trace the lines that cross through the middle of the figure from corner to corner, first the vertical line from top to bottom, then the horizontal line from left to right. Finally, trace around each of the four triangles defined by the figure in turn, both clockwise and counterclockwise. Do this all in your mind with your eyes closed.

Remember not to strain any part of your body. Keep the muscles around your eyes relaxed. Do not tense up your jaw or neck, and be aware of your abdominal and thigh muscles. These areas are particularly prone to tense up gradually as these concentration exercises are worked.

To end the exercise, open your eyes and take a few silent breaths.

Exercise 5.9: Mental Manipulation of the Tetragram

Adopt the sitting posture and take a few silent breaths to prepare. Close your eyes. Visualize the figure of the tetragram in glowing white lines on a black background—remember, it is a square tipped up on one corner so that it forms a diamond shape, with crossed lines running from its corners through its center. Hold the tetragram in your mind for a minute or so without allowing it to waver, while keeping your mind empty of all thoughts or other images.

Mentally remove one of the sides of the tetragram and hold the remaining parts of the figure in your mind for around a dozen seconds. Take away another side of the square, so that only two sides remain and hold the image. Take away the third side and contemplate the figure. Take away the final side of the square and contemplate the remaining crossed lines. Remove the left side of the horizontal line. Remove the right side, holding the image for a dozen seconds. Now take away the top half of the vertical line, and finally, take away the last part of the figure, the bottom half of the vertical line.

Continue to focus on the point where the crossed lines intersected for a minute or so. Be aware of the darkness and emptiness. Now reverse the steps you just went through, replacing the lower half of the vertical line, the upper half, the right side of the horizontal line, the left side, and successively the four sides of the square, until you have completely reconstructed the tetragram in your imagination. Remember to pause after each stage for a dozen seconds or so to contemplate the change.

The key to success is keeping your mind completely fixed on the figure in your imagination, allowing no extraneous thoughts or images to intrude and distract you. Concentrate on the rebuilt tetragram for a minute or two.

Open your eyes and take a few silent breaths to end the exercise.

Exercise 5.10: Concentration on Geometric Forms

This is one of my favorite exercises in concentration. I have been doing it for decades. It is described in several of my other books with slight variations. I sometimes perform it when I am lying in bed before sleep, but I don't recommend this to beginners, because it is too easy to lose focus and drift off to sleep if you do it while lying in bed.

Assume the sitting posture in a quiet place and take a few silent breaths to relax and focus your mind. Close your eyes. In the darkness of your closed eyelids, become aware of an unlimited space all around you that has nothing within it except the point of your own awareness. You float in this dark vastness without a body or form of any kind.

Imagine another point some distance away from you, floating in space. This point is infinitely small and featureless. It has no shape, no color, and no size, but nevertheless, you are aware of it. Hold your mind on only this dimensionless point.

Extend this point both upward and downward through the darkness an infinite distance, so that you are not aware of the ends of this line above or below. Hold this vertical line in your mind as you float in the darkness, contemplating it. It has no thickness and no color, but you are aware of its existence. Think of it as an infinitely thin black thread stretching up and down with no ends.

Extend a second line from your imagined point out to the sides. It crosses this vertical line at perfect right angles. Together, the two crossing lines define a vertical plane that is transparent and colorless. Allow your own point of awareness to cross through this plane, floating from one side to the other side, and contemplate it from both sides in turn.

Extend a third line horizontally out in both directions from the imagined point. This line is perfectly perpendicular to the vertical plane you have already defined. Together with the plane, it defines two new planes. All three planes cross at right angles through the original point, and they define eight regions of space that touch with their corners at the original point.

Hold these three crossing lines and the three planes they define in your mind, but try not to picture them with colors or thickness. The planes are perfectly transparent and colorless.

Now allow your awareness to float from one division of the darkness of space to another, crossing through the planes. Visit in turn all eight sectors of space, and hold in your mind the changing angles of the three intersecting planes from your perspective as you move from one sector to another.

This exercise may prove difficult at first, but with practice you will find yourself able to complete it in ten minutes. The act of holding something in your mind that has no color or dimension is particularly useful in strengthening your power of concentration.

When you are ready, open your eyes and take a few silent breaths to relax your mind.

DRAMATIZATION

When working magic, as you visualize in your mind the fulfillment of your purpose, you act out that purpose in some ritualized way. In traditional magic, this dramatization involves the use of physical instruments or materials, but the same result can be accomplished using only the mind and body.

By acting out the fulfillment of the ritual purpose in a symbolic way, we bring its achievement into the physical world that we usually believe ourselves to inhabit. This is what we like to call the "real world." It is no more real than the world of the imagination, only different, but due to our lifelong conditioning, we tend to consider it more important than what goes on in our mind. This conditioning is what gives the external dramatization of the ritual purpose its power. In magic, instead of fighting against it, we use it to our advantage by physically acting out the fulfillment of our purpose.

MAGIC RELIES ON DRAMATIZATION

All conventional systems of magic rely heavily on ritual dramatization. The magician lights candles, walks around the altar, draws sigils on paper, inscribes pentagrams on the air with the wand or the sword, and so on. The physical performance of the purpose fulfilling itself in a symbolic way helps to manifest that purpose.

The physical acting out of the fulfillment of the ritual purpose will not necessarily correspond with its visualized fulfillment. Both will have the same basic message, but their symbolism may differ. For example, you might visualize using a flaming sword to cut through a chain across your path, but you might at the same time extend your right arm and draw your hand down through the air with a slashing motion. Your hand and the imaginary sword both represent symbolically the same thing, the cutting of the barrier you wish to pass.

To increase its effectiveness, all ritual work should involve some external dramatization. It is true that you can do magic solely in your imagination, using your powers of visualization and concentration, but this is quite difficult. Dramatization makes it easier to do ritual work successfully.

Dramatization in magic is based on the occult principle of similarity or sympathy—that similar things are occultly connected, and that by manipulating one thing, you can affect through magic the thing it resembles. The witch's poppet discussed in the first chapter provides an example. If a doll is made to resemble a human being and given characteristics of that person, such as baptizing the doll in the person's name or dressing the doll in the same way the person dresses, then through occult sympathy what is done to the doll can be made to happen to the person. A pin thrust through the leg of the doll will cause stabbing pain in the leg of the person.

When you act out an event while working magic, you have an inward understanding that the effect you wish to achieve is actually taking place, and if your concentration, visualization, and will are strong enough, the effect occurs through the sympathetic connection you have made between the dramatic action and the actual event.

NECTANEBUS

One of the rulers of ancient Egypt, Nectanebus, who was king around 358 BCE, is remembered in history as a great magician. When he wished the Egyptian navy to win a sea battle with an opposing navy, he would fill a large basin with water and place into it tiny wax models of ships representing both his navy and the naval force of his enemy. Then he would destroy the tiny model ships of his enemy's navy while leaving the models of his own ships unharmed. In this way, he is said to have achieved great naval victories.[4]

The writer known as Pseudo-Callisthenes romanticized this tale by asserting in the first chapter of his *History of Alexander the Great* that the little wax models would magically spring to life and fight a battle in the basin, with the models of the king prevailing over the models of the foe, but it is easy to see what was actually being done by Nectanebus.[5] He would dramatically enact the battle and enact the victory of his own navy by setting on fire or otherwise destroying the model ships representing the navy of his enemy.

---

4. E. A. Wallis Budge, *Egyptian Magic*, vol. 2, *Books on Egypt and Chaldea* (London: Kegan Paul, Trench, Trübner & Co., 1901), 91–93.
5. E. A. Wallis Budge, trans. and ed, *The History of Alexander the Great, Being the Syriac Version of the Pseudo-Callisthenes* (Cambridge, UK: Cambridge University Press, 1889), 1–2.

In the magic described in this book, our dramatizations will not approach this level of complexity. Even so, the skill must be practiced if you are to use it effectively. Dramatization in the form of body postures and hand gestures serves to invoke, focus, channel, project, and banish esoteric energies. These energies are sometimes known as *blind forces*, because they are like electricity—neither good nor evil in themselves, although they may be used for good or evil purposes.

The following exercises will help you learn how to control and direct the fundamental blind forces of magic. Not only dramatization but visualization and concentration are employed.

EXERCISES FOR CHAPTER 6

Exercise 6.1: Invoking Positive Energy

This exercise should be done during daylight hours under natural light. It may be done outdoors beneath the rays of the sun or indoors with the light coming through a window. The light does not need to be direct sunlight—you can do the exercise on a cloudy day. Choose a quiet location where you will not be disturbed.

Stand facing the east with your arms relaxed at your sides. The east is the direction of the rising sun, which brings warmth and light to the world. Take several slow, silent breaths to make your mind tranquil.

Become aware of the light in the air all around you. This solar radiation envelops you and presses against your body. It touches every pore and every tiny hair on your skin, even beneath your clothing, because infrared rays that are part of the sun's radiation can pass through clothing.

Raise your hands above your head so that your extended arms form a V shape. Turn your palms upward and spread your fingers slightly, as though catching raindrops on your palms. Tilt your face upward, but do not strain your neck. This posture should be easy and natural.

As you inhale through your nose for four slow mental beats, visualize both with your inner sight and your psychic sense of touch the radiant energy of the sun in the heavens being drawn down and concentrated in your hands. The esoteric aspect of this energy is not obstructed by walls or ceilings. As it concentrates itself, it becomes a vibrant golden color. Visualize this golden light flowing down your arms and into your chest. Visualize your chest as a hollow vessel that becomes filled with dancing eddies of light energy. You should imagine the light to be made up of countless tiny golden flecks that are like flecks of dust illuminated by sunlight.

Hold your lungs full of air for one beat as you lower your face to took directly forward. Close your hands into loose fists, cross your forearms at the wrists over your breast, and shut your eyes. Exhale silently through your nose for the same four-beat duration that you inhaled, and visualize the dancing golden light energy inside your hollow chest expanding throughout your body to fill your arms and legs. It extends from the crown of your head to the soles of your feet. The closing of your hands and the crossing of your wrists prevents the light energy from flowing out with your exhaled breath. Instead, this soothing, healing, vitalizing energy is locked inside your body.

Hold your lungs empty for a beat, then open your eyes, unclench your fists, look upward, and raise your arms once more above your head. Draw down the light of the sun into your hands for four slow beats as you inhale silently through the nose. Visualize the radiant energy flowing down your arms into your chest.

Repeat a dozen times or so this cycle of indrawing the light energy into your chest on the inhalation of your breath while standing with arms raised above your head, then expanding it throughout your body on the exhalation while standing with eyes shut and forearms crossed over your breast.

You may feel a bit lightheaded, so take care not to lose your balance. It is important never to overfill your lungs with air or to attempt to completely empty them. This accomplishes nothing and, if carried to an extreme degree, may even injure your lungs. There is no need to strain physically while doing this exercise—the effort should be mental. To end the exercise, stand with your arms at your sides as you take a few relaxed, silent breaths.

The purpose of this exercise is to energize you physically and sharpen your thoughts. You can perform it half a dozen times just before you have some difficult or unpleasant task to do, and the esoteric aspect of the solar energy accumulated inside your body will give you courage, clarity, and determination.

Exercise 6.2: Banishing Negative Energy

This exercise should be done after sunset. It may be done outdoors beneath the light of the moon, but it is not necessary to see the moon or even for the moon to be above the horizon to perform the exercise, only that it be done at night. If you do the exercise indoors, choose a quiet room or other location where you will not be disturbed, and turn out the room lights. This is an excellent exercise to perform just before going to bed. It will relax both mind and body and help you fall quickly into a deep, refreshing sleep.

Adopt a standing posture facing west with your arms relaxed at your sides. Gaze at the unseen distant horizon. Draw a few silent breaths to focus your mind on what you are about to do.

Visualize with both your inner sight and your psychic sense of touch the fatigue that has built up in your body over the course of your day. You can imagine this as a brown cloud of tiredness and minor aches all through your body but concentrated in the hollow vessel of your chest. Visualize this fatigue and minor aching as very fine dust or smoke particles that eddy and swirl inside you.

Raise your arms in a V shape with your palms turned upward and tilt your face upward. Visualize the full moon above you, much larger than you normally see it, and glowing with silver light. Inhale for four slow beats through your nose, and as you do so, imagine pure, cool, soothing, lunar energy flowing down through your hands and arms into your chest. You should visualize this as a cloud of fine silver particles, like silver dust, that dances and spreads outward to all parts of your body, even to the tips of your fingers and toes.

Pause for only a single beat with your lungs full, then extend your arms downward at an angle at your sides so that they form an A shape with its apex at the top of your head, and turn down your palms. Exhale for four slow beats while you visualize the cooling, lunar energy with which you filled yourself flushing out the swirling eddies of brown fatigue dust and body aches. Visualize the dull, dirty brown fatigue energy in your chest flowing down both your arms and pouring out the palms of your hands like streams of fine dust, to fall through the floor into the earth below your feet. It streams into the ground from the downturned palms of your hands along with the dancing silver particles of the moon.

Repeat this cycle of drawing down through your upraised hands cooling lunar energy from the moon while you inhale for slow four beats, then expelling your fatigue for four beats with your arms extended downward at an angle, the palms turned down, as you exhale for four beats. It is vital that you strongly visualize the flow of silver lunar particles through your body as you do so. Do the exercise a dozen times or so, or until you have a sense that all the fatigue has been flushed from your body, leaving you cleansed and purified by the cooling lunar light.

Adopt a standing posture with arms relaxed at your sides, and contemplate your inner condition while taking several silent breaths to end the exercise.

Exercise 6.3: Concentrating Energy with a Spiral

Face east in a standing posture and take a few silent breaths to calm your thoughts.

Raise your arms in a posture of invocation so that they form the sides of a V. Gaze upward through the ceiling into the heavens and visualize a vortex of light begin to form in the air above you. See it as a turning disk of bluish-white light that looks something like the disk of a rotating galaxy. It rotates in a counterclockwise direction as you gaze up at it. With the power of your will, draw it nearer until it is between your hands.

Slowly, lower your arms and bring them closer together in front of you, drawing down this vortex between your outstretched hands. Feel the edges of this turning spiral of energy with your fingers and the palms of your hands. It will feel slightly electric, and the hairs on the backs of your hands will stand up the way they do when charged with static.

Bring your hands closer together, and as you do so, use the force of your will to compress the vortex into a spinning ball of blue-white energy, so that it becomes smaller and smaller between your cupped palms. When your cupped palms touch, draw them in to your chest. Feel the ball spinning counterclockwise between your palms. It is now warm, but not unpleasantly so.

Draw a deep breath. As you exhale your breath forcefully through your mouth with an audible huff, step forward on your right leg and at the same time thrust your arms forward, opening your palms and turning them forward to thrust the ball of energy away from you. For those who are sports-minded, the motion is similar to a chest pass in basketball. Push the ball of energy away with the palms of your hands, with the sharp exhalation of your breath, and with the power of your will. Visualize it flying toward the horizon, getting smaller and smaller until it is lost from view.

Step back with your right foot and lower your arms to your sides to resume the standing posture. Draw a few silent breaths to end the exercise.

Exercise 6.4: Energy Charging

This charging may be done with any form of esoteric energy for a wide variety of purposes. The energy of the five occult elements—spirit, fire, air, water, and earth—is suitable for practice. I will describe the manipulation of the elemental quintessence of spirit or light because it is benign in nature, but this exercise can be done with any of the elements or, indeed, with any other esoteric energy.

Find an object into which you wish to project esoteric energy. A bowl of water is a good choice, because the charged water can then be used to energize and heal the body, by bathing an injured or sick part with the water or by drinking the water. If kept in a sealed vessel in a dark, cool place, charged water will retain its virtue for several days.

You may, if you wish, choose a physical object such as a stone, a statuette, a ring, a pendant, a mirror, a picture, a knife, or whatever you wish to charge with energy. Whatever object you select, it must be compatible with the energy you project into it. For example, a bowl of water would be a poor choice to charge with the force of elemental fire, because the elements fire and water conflict.

The object or substance to be charged should be elevated on a table or shelf and about six feet away from you. Begin in a standing posture facing the object.

Draw down a counterclockwise spiral of light or spirit energy and compress it into a ball between your cupped palms, as you did in the previous exercise. Take a deep breath. Focus your will upon the blue-white ball of spirit energy between your hands. As you exhale strongly and audibly through your mouth with a huffing sound, step forward on your right leg and thrust the ball of energy away from you with your palms into the thing you seek to charge. In this example, it is a small glass bowl of water. Use the combined force of your breath, the motion of your body and hands, and the power of your will to project the energy ball from your body.

Visualize the energy ball strike the bowl of water. As it strikes, the energy fills the bowl and covers it, making it glow with a dancing blue-white radiance that is quickly absorbed. Visualize a residual glow on the surface of the water.

Step back and lower your arms in a relaxed standing posture. Turn your mind completely away from what you have just done. Don't try not to think about it, because that is impossible, but hold in the back of your mind the quiet assurance that the water has been charged with the energy of spirit. Hold it in your mind as a thing that has been accomplished and is in the past and, therefore, need not be worried about because it cannot be changed.

Take a few silent breaths to relax and end the exercise.

Exercise 6.5: Projecting a Circle

In this exercise, you will practice projecting and absorbing a magic circle that is composed of the energy of elemental spirit, the quintessence that underlies all things.

Adopt a standing posture facing east in an open space on your floor in a room where you will not be disturbed. Take a few silent breaths to focus your mind.

Press your left palm flat against the center of your chest, and extend your right arm straight out in front of you at the level of your heart, pointing with your index finger.

In the center of your chest, be aware of your own vital energies expressed by the beating of your heart and the breathing of your lungs. Mentally gather and concentrate the vital energy throughout your whole body into a ball of soft white fire, and visualize it glowing with power beneath your left palm. Make it about the size of a baseball.

Using your will, cause a stream of white fire to flow from this ball into your left palm, up your left arm, across your shoulders, along your right arm, and out through the extended index finger of your right hand, so that you can see it upon the air with your inner vision.

Slowly turn on your own axis where you stand in a clockwise direction, projecting the stream of white fire onto the air like a line of ink from a fountain pen on a sheet of paper, so that it forms a flaming ring around you at the level of your heart. Project it a foot or two beyond your fingertip. Join the end of the circle with its beginning when you have turned a full rotation. The fiery white circle floats on the air at the level of your heart.

Resume the standing posture facing east. Hold this unbroken circle of soft white fire in your imagination, and try to make it as real to your senses as you can. See it flickering in the air as though it were a flaming lasso. Hear the flutter of the flames. Feel their gentle warmth as the fire radiates energy.

You can expand or contract this circle with the power of your will. Press against it on all sides with your will to make it larger, then pull it inward with your will to make it smaller, before returning it to its original size.

When you have sustained this circle for a minute or two, extend your left arm in front of you at heart level while pointing with the left index finger, and hold your right palm pressed flat against the center of your chest. Mentally break the circle of flaming white spirit energy and begin to draw one side of it into the tip of your left index finger as you slowly rotate your body in a counterclockwise direction on the spot where you stand. Keep turning your body to complete a full rotation on your axis so that the whole of the flaming circle is drawn up your left arm, across your shoulders, down your right arm, and through your right palm into the center of your chest.

Once again, assume the standing posture facing east. Contemplate the flaming ball of soft white fire in the center of your chest, then allow it to expand and spread throughout your entire body. It has a soothing, healing virtue that makes the nerves tingle in your arms and legs.

Take several silent breaths to end the exercise.

Exercise 6.6: Pillar of Light

Adopt a standing posture facing east and take several silent breaths to calm and focus your mind. Become aware of the stars that are always present above you, day or night.

Bring your feet together and raise your hands straight above your head, pressing your palms together with your fingers pointing upward. Your arms will be close to your ears on both sides, but do not hunch your shoulders. Keep your shoulders relaxed.

Use the power of your will to draw down the blue-white energy of the stars into your joined hands. Do this rhythmically, in time with audible inhalations. As you audibly inhale through your mouth with a whooshing sound, focus your attention on your hands and draw down celestial energy into them. As you silently exhale through your nose, maintain your mental focus on the ball of energy surrounding your hands. Do a dozen repetitions or so until your hands are strongly charged.

Press the fingers of your left hand flat to your forehead and the fingers of your right hand flat to your lower belly below your navel.

As you audibly inhale through your pursed lips, draw blue-white celestial energy straight upward from your right hand along your spine into your head. As you audibly exhale, send the energy sliding down from your left hand in a serpentine path that runs down your left arm, across your shoulders, and down your right arm to your lower belly.

Continue in this way, slowly inhaling and exhaling in an audible way while pulling celestial energy up your spine, and then allowing it to flow back down the serpentine path of your two arms.

After two or three dozen cycles, draw the energy to the top of your head with an audible inhalation. Raise both hands above your head with the palms turned upward. Exhale forcefully through your mouth and use the power of your will to send a pulse of blue-white energy through the top of your head and straight upward into the heavens, where it dissipates among the stars.

Lower your arms to your sides and assume a standing posture. Take a few silent breaths to relax and end the exercise.

Exercise 6.7: Expanding Your Astral Body

In this dramatization exercise, you will expand your astral body. This is the form of yourself you project into the astral world and the way you look to spiritual beings when they see you. Usually, it looks exactly like your physical body, but know that you have the latent ability to take full control over it and over the way you present yourself in the astral realms to the spirits who dwell there.

Face the east in the standing posture. Take several silent breaths to calm your mind. Close your eyes.

Become aware of your astral body. It penetrates your physical body and is the same size and shape as your physical body. If you cannot actually sense it within you, use the power of visualization to picture it. Feel it as a very subtle pressure inside the entire surface of your skin. It penetrates your bones, your muscles, your organs—every part of your physical body.

Press your palms together in front of your chest in a gesture of prayer. Take a deep breath, and as you slowly and audibly exhale, widen your stance and extend your arms straight out to the sides, pushing with the palms of your hands outward. Use your will to push in all directions as you extend your arms to the sides with your palms turned out. Time the full extension of your arms to correspond with the exhalation of your breath.

As you extend your arms, visualize the walls, floor, and ceiling of the room in which you stand come apart and fly away in all directions. See yourself standing on an endless beach of flat sand with the ocean in front of you. It is night, and the sky above is filled with stars.

With your lungs held empty, see in your mind your astral body, arms spread wide, standing on the sand. Begin to inhale a slow, deep breath, and as you do so, close your hands into fists and bring them inward, at last crossing them at the wrists in front of your chest. Hold your lungs filled with air. Use the force of your will to expand your astral form. Continue to use your will to make your astral body larger and larger, until the sand beneath you is far below and your head is among the stars.

Let the entire globe of the world drop away beneath your feet so that your astral form floats in space, surrounded by stars. It is now so large that there are stars inside your astral body as well as outside. Contemplate your gigantic astral form for half a minute or so while retaining your breath.

When you have held your aura expanded with your lungs filled, exhale audibly through your mouth with a whooshing sound as you open your fists and lower your hands at your sides, pushing downward with your palms. Visualize your astral body shrinking like a balloon from which the air is gradually released. As your astral form reunites with your physical body, will the walls, ceiling, and floor of the room to come flying back together.

Unite your palms in a gesture of prayer in front of your chest, and be aware that your astral body has returned to its usual place within your physical body. Lower your arms to your sides and assume a standing posture. Take a few silent breaths to end the exercise.

Exercise 6.8: Channeling Energy

In this exercise, you will practice channeling the esoteric energy of the stars through your body. The energy is drawn down from the heavens and directed through your body into the earth beneath you. Your body acts as a kind of circuit through which this force flows, the way electrical potential flows along a copper wire.

Adopt the standing posture facing east in a quiet place where you will not be disturbed. Look directly forward into infinity, disregarding anything in your field of vision. Be aware of what is happening inside you. Take several silent breaths to calm and focus your mind.

Raise your left hand high above your head, and at the same time, point downward with your right hand toward the floor. Continue to gaze straight ahead at the unseen horizon, but direct your attention mentally to the heavens above you. Project your awareness through the ceiling and beyond the envelope of air that surrounds this planet, out among the vastness of the stars.

With the power of your will, draw down the blue-white energy of this starry celestial sphere into your left hand, which acts as a kind of lightning rod. Inhale slowly and audibly as you attract this energy. Feel it tingle in your hand and flow down your left arm into your chest, where it circles in a counterclockwise swirl.

As you exhale slowly and audibly, use your will to direct this energy swirling in your chest down your right arm and out from your right hand in the form of a stream of blue-white energy that is like electricity.

Repeat this cycle of audible breaths a dozen times or so. Your heart rate will increase slightly. This is not dangerous. The raw celestial energy you are drawing through your body is not of a harmful nature. It will cleanse and purify you.

When you have channeled this celestial energy for several minutes, shift into a standing posture with both arms at your sides. Take a few silent breaths to end the exercise.

Exercise 6.9: Charging Objects

Find some small personal object you wish to practice with and place it on a table or desk in a quiet place where you can work undisturbed. It can be anything you carry close to you—a piece of jewelry, a small stone you keep for good luck, a ring, an article of clothing, a pocketknife, a photograph, a pen.

The nature of celestial fire is to purify and energize. It is good for cleansing atmospheres, banishing depression, dispelling dark or obsessive thoughts, increasing vitality, and sharpening mental focus. The object you will charge in this exercise will retain a portion of celestial energy for a few days, but it will gradually decline until it is gone. Stone will hold this charge much longer than any other material.

Assume a standing posture in front of the object. It is good if you can face east while doing this exercise, but it is not essential. East is the direction of the dawn, which symbolizes beginning. Take a few silent breaths to prepare.

Raise your left hand high above your head. Hold your right hand pressed over the object. Direct your gaze forward at the unseen distant horizon, but send your awareness upward through the ceiling into the darkness of space between the stars.

Use the force of your will to draw down celestial fire into your left hand. Your left arm and hand act as a lightning rod for this energy, which should be visualized as bright white with a hint of blue. Inhale slowly and audibly through your mouth as you channel this energy down your left arm and into your chest.

Exhale slowly and audibly between your pursed lips as you visualize the energy moving from your chest into your right arm and exiting from your right palm into the object.

Remember, when you inhale, you are pulling energy; when you exhale, you are pushing energy. Repeat this cycle of inward and outward audible breaths until you sense that the object cannot hold any more of this blue-white charge.

Relax your hands, lower your arms to your sides, and adopt a standing posture. As you hold this posture for a minute or so while breathing normally, in your mind's eye see the object glow with esoteric energy. Take several silent breaths to end the exercise.

Exercise 6.10: Five Lamps

If you are in poor physical condition, this exercise may be slightly taxing, only because it requires that you hold your arms extended at your sides for several minutes without moving or lowering them. If you find that your arms are aching or become too tired, you may shorten the stages of the exercise and also bend your elbows slightly to relieve the strain.

Assume a standing posture facing east and take a few silent breaths to calm your mind.

Spread your legs and your arms wide so that your hands, your feet, and the crown of your head roughly define the five points of an upright pentagram. Direct your gaze forward.

With the power of your will, draw down the blue-white celestial energy of the stars and concentrate it just above your head. Visualize a glowing sphere of translucent, blue-white light forming there. It is around a foot in diameter and touches you on the very top of your skull. Feel the contact as a slight tickling or itching on your scalp where the sphere touched your skin. It is electrical but not unpleasant. Take several slow breaths as you contemplate it.

With a slow, audible exhalation, direct some of the blue-white energy in the sphere in a ray downward at an angle to your right foot. The ray of light is able to pass through your right shoulder without being hindered. Inhale through your nose silently as you visualize a ball of translucent red energy around your right foot so that it encloses your entire foot. Feel the warmth of this energy on the skin of your foot. It is like the pleasant, warm glow from a fireplace. Contemplate this red ball for several breaths.

With an audible exhalation, cast another straight ray of energy from the red ball upward at an angle to your left hand. This ray is red in color, but it forms a bright, translucent yellow ball that completely surrounds your extended left hand. Take a few moments to visualize this yellow sphere of energy as you inhale silently through your nose, and feel its pressure around your palm and fingers like the touch of a warm spring breeze against your skin.

Exhaling slowly and audibly through your mouth, send a ray of yellow energy straight through your shoulders to your right hand. The ray is able to pass through your body without being hindered. It forms a translucent, blue ball around your right hand. The energy of the blue ball is cooling and soothing as it washes over your skin. Contemplate this blue ball as you inhale slowly and silently through your nose.

Exhaling audibly, cause a ray of blue energy to travel from the blue ball around your right hand directly to your left foot, where it forms a translucent, dark-green sphere around your foot. The pressure of the energy in the green sphere is cool and somewhat heavy, but not uncomfortably so. It encloses your left foot on all sides. Take a slow, silent inhalation through your nose as you visualize it clearly, and feel this pressure and coolness.

As you exhale audibly through your mouth, use your will to direct a green ray from the green ball around your left foot upward at an angle to the white sphere above your head so that it enters the white sphere. It does not change the color of the white sphere. Inhaling silently, reinforce in your mind the five colored spheres and the five colored rays that link them together.

In one general movement of your body, draw your legs together and press your palms together in front of your chest in a prayer posture. As you make this contraction of your body, mentally draw the four colored balls of energy around your hands and feet into the center of your chest, and send their combined energies upward into the fifth white ball that is still above your head.

Smoothly raise your hands directly above the top of your head with your palms turned upward. As you make this motion with your hands, use the force of your will to push the white sphere straight upward through the ceiling of your room, through the roof of the building you occupy, and beyond the atmosphere of Earth into the darkness of the space between the stars, where its energy expands and dissipates.

Lower your arms to your side and adopt a standing posture. Draw several silent breaths to end the exercise.

INCANTATION

Can rituals be done without saying anything at all? Of course they can, but even a silent ritual has a purpose that you must be able to articulate in your mind in the form of words. Unless you can express your purpose to yourself clearly and simply enough to state it in a brief sentence, you probably don't understand your purpose well enough to ever achieve it.

You may not say out loud during the actual ritual process, "Doing these actions will achieve [such and such a purpose]," but this is what must be in the back of your mind. At the most basic level, incantation is the ritual intention expressed as words, whether silently in the head or out loud on the breath. Prayer, chants, and words of power all support this articulated intention.

An incantation must be expressed as a purpose realized. You do not say to yourself, for example, "By this action, I wish to find a good job," but rather you say, "By this action, I find a good job." To take another example, you don't say to yourself, "I do this to overcome my fear of snakes," you say to yourself, "Doing this overcomes my fear of snakes."

While you act out the symbolic achievement of your ritual purpose in a dramatic way, with movements, postures, and gestures, you also utter aloud a statement or series of statements expressing that purpose fulfilled. This is a common practice of traditional magic. The wisewoman or cunning man speaks the fulfillment of the purpose with the firm belief that the magic of the words makes it so.

Folk magic is filled with simple spoken charms for such things as removing warts, curing sickness, gaining a lover, hurting an enemy, and the like. Of course, in themselves, these little spoken charms are not effective. They must be supported by visualization, concentration, dramatization, and an underlying conviction on both the conscious and subconscious levels that the magic will succeed.

Traditionally, magicians use words of power in their incantations. These are words believed by magicians to possess a special efficacy in achieving the ritual purpose. By the magician vibrating them aloud on the breath, the ritual is energized. It is not necessary when working modern magic to use ancient barbarous words from the grimoires, although these often serve quite well. Modern magicians will select modern words of power that support their intentions. As is so often the case in life, belief in a thing tends to make it so. The very belief the magician has in the force of the words lends them magical efficacy.

VIBRATING INCANTATIONS ALOUD

How an incantation is uttered is important in traditional magic. The magical system of the Golden Dawn has an elaborate method for vibrating words and names of power on the breath, using the diaphragm, chest, throat, and mouth to make them resonate and boom out upon the air. The effect can be startling to those who do not expect it. Correctly vibrated words roll forth like thunder and are compelling, not only to any spirits that may be present but to other human beings.

The physical act of vibrating words is accompanied in the Golden Dawn method by a specific visualization. The word of power to be vibrated is imagined written on the heart in brilliant letters of blazing white light. The magician also imagines that the words vibrated spread to the far reaches of the universe.

It is not absolutely necessary to vibrate your incantations. I seldom use the Golden Dawn method in my own work because it is so *loud*. It is also, in my opinion, unnecessarily theatrical, which is not to be wondered at, since the Hermetic Order of the Golden Dawn was founded by Freemasons accustomed to highly elaborate and theatrical rituals.

Incantations can, if required by circumstance, be uttered under the breath, so that they are almost or wholly inaudible to others. It was often the case in ancient times that magicians wished to avoid detection when they spoke their spells. They would mutter them so that no person passing could understand what they were saying, even if they heard the mutter.

It was this custom that gave rise to the famous Biblical verse, "Seek unto them that have familiar spirits, and unto wizards that peep, and that mutter" (Isaiah 8:19).[6] The mention of peeping, by the way, refers to the evil eye, which witches and wizards were believed to cast when they looked at someone askance, or from the corners of their eyes.

Generally, the best result will be achieved when incantations are spoken clearly in a confident tone. The vowel sounds should

6. King James Version.

resonate within your chest. You do not need to shout to achieve this resonance. The force of the words comes from the openness of the chest and throat. Practice makes perfect. You will know you are doing it the right way when you feel a tickling sensation in your throat, a buzzing in your nose and sinuses, and a reverberation in your chest as you vibrate the words of your incantations.

If you are in a situation where others are close by and you do not wish them to hear you, resort to the method of the ancient wizards and sound the words sub-vocally in your throat, so that only a whisper or a murmur comes from your mouth. If you have need for total silence, it will be enough to speak your incantations mentally, so that they resonate aloud only in your imagination.

You should experiment with these three manners of incantation—vibrating the words aloud, murmuring or whispering them under your breath, and sounding them only in your own mind—so that you can incant with the method that best suits the circumstances in which you find yourself.

PURPOSES OF INCANTATION

Incantation is used to define clearly and explicitly the reason you are working magic. Unless you can state your purpose in a few words, you don't understand it yourself, and if you don't understand it, nothing will be achieved. Incantation is a way of proclaiming both to your higher self and to the spirits of the earthly and heavenly spheres exactly what you intend.

For example, if you are performing a ritual to cleanse a room of its baleful or depressing atmosphere, you would speak at the outset something like this: "By this working, I cleanse and purify this space, banishing from it all hurtful forces." You might add to this statement of purpose a name of power as your authority:

"By this working, in the name of the mighty archangel Michael, I cleanse and purify this space."

Incantation is also used to describe in words the dramatic actions of the ritual. As you perform a ritual action, it can help to reinforce it by voicing what you are doing and your intention for doing it. If you were burning a written charm in order to realize the purpose for which it was made, you might speak the words "By this burning I send forth the power of this charm upon the four winds to the realization of its purpose."

Remember, you never state your incantations in such a way that you are asking for the fulfillment of an action; you always state them as though something has already been realized. You would never say, "I do this ritual because I want to find my lost ring." At first sight, this statement seems positive, but it really is not. Whenever you say "I want" you are saying that you do not have. That's the actual meaning of the word *want*—to want is to lack. Instead, you would express your intention in words something like "By the working of this ritual, my lost ring is found."

USE OF RHYME

Incantations were often expressed in rhyme in ancient times. We see an echo of this very real custom in Shakespeare's tragic play *Macbeth*, where in the opening scene of the fourth act, the three witches chant in rhyming verse around their cauldron.

> Eye of newt, and toe of frog,
> Wool of bat, and tongue of dog,
> Adder's fork, and blind-worm's sting,
> Lizard's leg, and howlet's wing,

For a charm of powerful trouble,
Like a hell-broth boil and bubble.[7]

There are many spoken charms or incantations recorded from folklore. They have no special power in themselves, but they illustrate to the modern magician a practical technique for composing incantations that are potent and enduring in the mind. To cite a single example that was used in Scotland to take away toothache:

Mars, hur, abursa, aburse.
Jesu Christ for Marys sake,
Take away this tooth-ach.[8]

In Christian folk magic, the names of God, angels, and saints often appear as names of power to grant authority to the incantation. There is a double authority being used here. The magician calls upon the authority of Jesus to compel the ache to go away, but he also calls upon the authority of merciful and loving Mary to urge Jesus to act. The first line of the charm appears to consist of what are known as *barbarous words of power*—words whose meaning is unknown to those who speak them but that are believed to possess occult potency.

THE WORDING OF INCANTATIONS

The wording of the toothache charm is a little wrong, from a magical point of view—the third line should read "Takes away this tooth-ach." To chant "take away" is to ask Jesus for relief, but to chant "takes away" is to state emphatically that Jesus is taking away the pain. This charm was written out three times on slips of paper,

---

7. William Shakespeare, *Macbeth,* 4.1.14–19.

8. Aubrey, *Miscellanies*, 107.

which were successively read aloud and then cast into a fire. As the papers burned and the words vanished, so by sympathetic magic did the toothache.

The general rule for incantations is that they should be simple, brief, clear, positive statements. If they rhyme, so much the better. The authority of various angels and gods may be called upon in incantations to empower them, but be aware that before calling on the name of a god or spirit, the magician must be worthy to invoke that being. A malicious, dishonorable, and insincere man is wasting his time if he calls upon Jesus or Mary to enforce the fulfillment of his magic. They will not heed his call.

Traditional incantations can be efficacious in modern magic, but it is even more effective when you compose your own incantations that express the fulfillment of your purpose. Nothing is more personal than your own words, spoken from the heart.

The following exercises contain examples of the use of incantation in simple works of magic involving both the blind forces of nature and spirits. You can do these purely as exercises, but they are also practical rituals designed to achieve various useful purposes. The incantations are given as workable examples, but you do not need to follow them slavishly. I encourage you to compose your own incantations.

EXERCISES FOR CHAPTER 7

Exercise 7.1: To End a Headache

Assume the sitting posture facing east in a quiet room. The room should be dimly lit, with the curtains closed during the day or the lights turned low if it is night. There must be no distractions. Take a few silent breaths to calm your mind.

Put your palms together in a gesture of prayer in front of your face and tilt your head slightly forward. Press the upper part of your forehead against your two thumbs between the first and second knuckle. You will find that the curve of your skull fits quite comfortably against this part of your thumbs. Relax your neck and allow your hands to support the weight of your head. Close your eyes.

Visualize a small bird with bright red feathers inside your hollow skull. The bird is pecking at the walls of its prison and fluttering around in a frantic effort to escape. Try to feel the bird inside your head. Draw a deep breath, hold it for a beat or two, then speak these words:

Bird of pain in cage of bone,
The door is open, fly away **home.**

As you say the final word with emphasis, forcefully exhale the remaining air from your lungs and open your eyes wide. At the same time, separate your hands, throwing them forward on extended arms directly away from your face with the fingers spread wide so that you can look between your hands. Visualize the bird flying away from you on rapidly fluttering red wings, and hold the awareness that it carries your pain away with it.

Close your eyes and resume the sitting posture, with your hands on your knees. Be aware that your pain is now separate from your head. You can still feel it, but because it is not inside your head any longer, it has lost its power to hurt you. Breathe slow, regular breaths. Think of the red bird flying further and further away with each passing moment, and be aware that the further it goes, the less you can sense your pain.

The trick to this exercise is to project your pain out of your head. Once you put your pain outside your skull, it cannot hurt you any longer, even though you are still aware of it.

After resting for a minute with your eyes closed, open your eyes, draw a few deep, silent breaths, and stand up to end the exercise.

Exercise 7.2: To Find a Misplaced Possession

If you have forgotten where you put your keys, wallet, eyeglasses, pen, or any other item, perform this simple ritual to remember where you placed it.

Take a standing posture with arms at your sides, and breathe deeply and silently a few times to focus your intention. Raise your left hand in front of you with your elbow bent and your palm forward, fingers separated slightly. Gently press the fingertips of your right hand to your forehead.

Slowly walk through your house, or wherever you think you misplaced or dropped the lost object, and extend your awareness to your left hand, making it sensitive. Be aware of very fine changes in the sensation of your left palm as you hold it in front of you, and note the slight air currents that cool your skin.

Repeat the following incantation in a quiet voice over and over in a rhythmic way. Draw a deep breath and chant the words, emptying your lungs as you speak them. If necessary, you can pause after the first line to exhale partially so that your lungs are emptied when you have finished speaking the second line. Draw another deep breath and repeat. Keep your mind empty as you chant the words:

I set it down and left it there:
There it sits, remember where.

Chant it softly to yourself with your attention on your left hand. When you come near the lost object, your left palm will feel different. It will probably be a tickling or crawling sensation. If you walk away from the object, this feeling will diminish. At some point the memory of where you put the object will jump back into your mind.

In this way, you can use your left hand as a kind of built-in dowsing rod to locate anything you may have lost. Do this exercise anytime you lose or misplace something, and don't be discouraged if you seem to have no success at first. It is a skill that must be learned through practice.

Exercise 7.3: To Banish Fears

This is a good exercise to perform if you have a buildup of general anxiety or if you are worried about something you must do or face in the near future—for example, if you have a public speaking engagement coming up. It is also good against phobias such as the fear of the dark, enclosed spaces, spiders, clowns, dogs, or whatever you may be afraid of.

Adopt the standing posture in a quiet place facing east. It is best if you have no distractions for your eyes or ears. Take a few silent breaths, then recite this incantation to yourself:

Fear is a black dog that barks in the night;
The dog runs away, the dog fears the light.

Raise both your arms above your head so that they form a V, with the palms turned upward in an invoking posture. Draw a slow, audible breath through your mouth that fills your lungs as you visualize the celestial light of the stars streaming down upon your palms and upon your upturned face. This light flows down into your body and fills your chest with blue-white radiance. Retain your breath with your lungs filled for a few moments as you visualize this light swirling inside your body, then speak these words:

The white light comes to stay.

Lower your arms into a banishing posture so they form an A-shape that has its point at your head, with your palms directed downward toward the floor, your face turned downward. As you do so, exhale audibly through your mouth in a smooth, controlled manner most of the remaining breath you have held. Visualize the blackness of your fear driven down your arms by the force of the light, so that the blackness streams out your palms through the floor and into the ground below it. As you visualize the fear leaving you, with the last part of your exhaled breath, speak these words:

The black dog runs away.

Raise your arms in the invoking posture and repeat the visualization of the light descending into your hands and head and filling your torso, as you inhale audibly through your pursed lips. Retain your breath with your lungs full for a second or two, then repeat the words "The white light comes to stay." Lower your hands in the banishing posture and visualize the blackness of your fear streaming out your palms into the earth below you as you exhale audibly from your lips. With the last of your breath, speak the words "The black dog runs away."

Repeat this sequence a dozen times or so, filling yourself with cosmic light from the heavens and flushing the darkness of your fear out of your mind and body into the earth. Use your breath and the sounds of your inhalation and exhalation to aid you in your visualization.

To end the exercise, return to the standing posture and take a few silent breaths to relax your mind.

Exercise 7.4: To Improve the Memory

This is a useful incantation to do if you have an upcoming examination or if you are trying to memorize something. Adopt the sitting posture and take a few silent breaths to relax and focus. Close your eyes.

Hold the facts you wish to remember clearly in your mind and visualize yourself standing in front of a display cabinet with glass doors. Create a symbolic image of the information you need to remember in the form of something you can hold in your hand. For example, you might wish to remember the date and details of the Battle of Agincourt for a history examination. For this, you might visualize yourself holding a beautiful little model of an English bowman drawing back the string of his longbow, about to loose an arrow at the French.

Hold the image of the little model in your mind, and feel its weight and texture with your fingers as you mentally turn it this way and that, admiring its craftsmanship. Then carefully place it on a shelf in the glass display case and close the door. As you do so, incant these words:

This memory I file away,
and in there it will stay
until I need it back, and then
I draw it out again.

Open your eyes, take a few silent breaths, and stand up to end the exercise.

Whenever you need to recover the information about the Battle of Agincourt that you previously studied and memorized, close your eyes and visualize yourself back in the same room with the display case. Go to the display case, open the glass door, and take out the model. As you look at the bowman and handle it in your imagination, the things you wished to remember will come back into your mind.

You can use the same imaginary room to remember numerous things this way. Each object you create should be associated with a single fact or a group of closely connected facts. If you fill up one display case with objects of memory, just imagine a second display case in the room. You can furnish the memory room with as many display cases as you need.

Exercise 7.5: To Prevent Nightmares

Nightmares are not a problem when they occur only occasionally, but it sometimes happens that when you start to study magic, the changes that take place in your deep mind will cause frequent bad dreams for a period of weeks or months. This has been likened to stirring up the muck that usually lies at the bottom of a pond. The subconscious part of your mind is awakened when you study magic, and what lies in its depths may rise to the surface. If you find that you are having more nightmares than you wish to have, you can work a simple ritual and speak an incantation to put a stop to them.

When you are ready to go to bed, stand quietly facing east in the standing posture. Take a few silent breaths to calm your thoughts.

Shift into a posture of prayer, with your hands pressed together in front of your chest and your head bowed. Close your eyes and visualize an old woman in rags riding along a forest path upon a gray horse that is little more than skin and bone. Both woman and horse have an evil look about them. Suddenly, an angel in a white robe, with multicolored, feathered wings folded on his back, steps forward to face the old woman. In his hands, he holds a spear covered down its whole length with rippling orange and yellow flames. He holds the spear crosswise before himself to bar the passage of the old woman. As he does so, recite this incantation:

The hag comes riding on her mare;
She meets an angel without fear.
He bars her path with flaming spear;
She turns and flies away from there.
Fly away, hag! Fly away, mare!
Be not there! Come not here!

As you speak the final word of the incantation, throw your hands forward and outward with your fingers spread wide. Visualize the old woman turn her horse around and gallop away down the path until she is lost from your inner sight between the trees of the forest.

Resume the standing posture with arms at your sides. Open your eyes and draw a few silent breaths to end the exercise. Go to bed and have sweet dreams.

Exercise 7.6: To Induce a Prophetic Dream

Sometimes, when we need guidance and are unsure which course we should follow, it can be useful to seek a greater understanding of the issue by inviting a prophetic dream. These dreams were often induced in ancient times both by pagans and by the early Christians. There were special places in the ancient world that pilgrims, both pagan and Christian, visited for the purpose of inducing prophetic dreams.

Prepare for your dream by showering or taking a bath and putting on clean sleepwear, if you wear clothing while you sleep. Prior to this, you should change your sheets and pillowcase so that you are sleeping on fresh sheets. Do not eat anything for five or six hours before going to bed, and drink only a moderate amount of water during that time, if you are thirsty.

It is best that your sleeping place be completely dark and silent. This is not always possible, but you should eliminate what light and sounds you can. Lie in your bed on your back, eyes closed, with your arms at your sides, your hands open, and your fingers relaxed.

Send your awareness upward through your ceiling and through the roof of your house into the night sky, higher and higher, until you drift in the silent blackness of space between the stars. Focus your attention upon the brightest star and recite this incantation to the Spirit of Creation in whatever form you conceive that Spirit.

Holy Spirit, source of light,
Come to me in sleep this night;
Shine in darkness, guide my way,
Send a dream ere break of day.

When you finish saying these words, relax and assume your usual sleeping posture. Do not think about what you have just said or about the prophetic dream you wish to invoke. Empty your mind of anxiety or expectation of any kind.

If you wake during the night with the memory of a dream, immediately write down as many details as you can remember before going back to sleep. You should keep a pad and pen beside your bed for this purpose. You may find yourself waking several times with dreams in your mind. Write them all down. They are all significant.

The information in the dreams will be in the form of symbolism that must be interpreted when you are fully awake. Don't worry about what the dreams mean when you wake up in the night; just write down everything you can remember as accurately as possible, and consider it the next day.

Exercise 7.7: To Bring Good Fortune

This little incantation can be used daily to improve the general good fortune in your life. Spoken daily, it will have a cumulative effect, and you will find that good things are happening more often than bad things, and that you are receiving sudden unexpected strokes of luck.

It's best to recite it at the same time each day, in a quiet place when you are alone and unobserved. Do not talk about it to others or reveal it to them. It is a private matter between you and the Roman goddess Fortuna.

Assume a standing posture in a quiet place facing the east, with your arms at your sides. Take a few silent breaths to calm and focus your mind.

Raise your arms high above your head in a gesture of invocation so that they form the two sides of a V shape. Close your eyes and visualize a beautiful woman with blue eyes and long golden hair, who wears a white dress, the hem of which falls to her feet. Her arms are bare. She holds between her hands a golden wheel with twelve golden spokes. As you look at the wheel, you see that it is revolving in a clockwise direction. The woman is aware of your attention. She smiles at you in a kindly and gracious manner.

Holding this visualization in your mind, recite these words, which you must memorize beforehand:

Loving Lady of the Wheel,
Turn my worry into bliss;
Upon my life, set your seal,
Mend my fortune with your kiss.

It turns my darkness into light;
It drives away the cares of night.
Away is banished all my strife;
You smile on me and bless my life.

Visualize the Lady Fortuna nodding her head in acknowledgment of your incantation to win her favor. In your mind, see her approach and lean forward to kiss you gently on the forehead. Feel the touch of her lips. See her smile upon you.

Open your eyes and resume the standing posture. Take several silent breaths to clear your mind and end this exercise.

Exercise 7.8: To Invoke Your Guardian Spirit

In the ancient world, Socrates was famed far and wide as a philosopher, but he was even more famous as the possessor of a good daemon who watched over his life and warned him when he was about to make the wrong decision. So well-known was the daemon of Socrates that both the philosophers Plutarch (b. c. 46 CE) and Apuleius (b. 124 CE) wrote essays on the subject.[9]

Everyone has a good angel watching over them. You might prefer to think of it as your guardian spirit. Unlike Socrates, most people are not aware of this guardian. They are so distracted by external, material events and by their desires, urges, and fears, that they cannot perceive the attempts by their guardian to warn them and guide them.

When something inside you tells you that you should do something, and you disregard it and do something else, then later discover

9. Plutarch, "A Discourse Concerning Socrates's Daemon," in *Plutarch's Morals*, vol. 2 (Boston: Little, Brown, and Company, 1874), 378–423; Apuleius, *On the God of Socrates*, in *The Works of Apuleius* (London: H. G. Bohn, 1853), 350–73.

that the quiet inclination you felt was correct, that was your guardian angel trying to communicate with you.

The following incantation should be recited daily. It will help you become aware of the presence of your good angel.

Stand facing the east with arms at your sides, and take a few silent breaths to calm your mind. Raise your arms to transition smoothly into an invoking posture. Incline your face upward. Speak the following words with sincere longing and an open heart:

Loving Watcher of my days,
Guide my steps and light my ways;
Walk with me through darkest night,
Turn the darkness into light.

Extend your awareness upward and feel the descent of a cooling, soothing presence upon your face and shoulders. Draw this presence into your body with the power of your will. Feel the presence of your guardian within you.

Shift back into the standing posture with which you began the exercise, and take a few silent breaths to end it.

Exercise 7.9: To Derive a Sign from a Book

Bibliomancy is an ancient form of divination. It has been practiced by Jews and Christians for many centuries. When you seek guidance on any matter, you invoke a higher power and ask that you be granted a sign that will illuminate whatever question is troubling you. Then you open a book at random and drop your index finger onto the page. Whatever verse your finger points to is the response of this oracle.

The Bible is probably the best book for this divination because of its rich symbolism. *The Complete Works of Shakespeare* also serves very well as a book oracle. You may wish to experiment with the collected poetical works of Milton, Byron, Keats, Dickinson, or other poets. Milton's *Paradise Lost* will often yield good results, as will Dante's *Divine Comedy* and Homer's *Odyssey* and *Iliad*. The pagan Romans used the *Aeneid* of the poet Virgil, who was so well respected that during the Middle Ages, he acquired the reputation of a great magician.

It is useful to invoke a higher spiritual power by means of an incantation before opening the book to select a line. It can be a god, an angel, a saint, your guardian spirit, or your own higher self, but you should call upon an intelligence larger than yourself to guide your hand.

Take up the book you have chosen for your oracle and hold it in both hands pressed to your chest. Stand facing the east and gaze straight forward at the unseen horizon. Compose your mind with several silent breaths.

Think strongly about the matter on which you seek guidance. It is best to reduce the matter to a single, simple question, which you should hold in your thoughts for several silent breaths. Then, release the question and empty your mind, making it as still as a pool of water at twilight.

Speak aloud this incantation to the higher power you have decided to call upon for guidance in the book oracle:

Your lamp, my truth; your staff, my guide.
Read from this book; stand by my side.
You light the page, you point the way;
Your words transform my night to day.

Without thinking about the question, close your eyes and open the book, then slide your index finger down one of the pages until you feel an impulse to stop. Open your eyes and read the line of text just above the tip of your index finger. If it is a sentence that covers more than a single line, accept the entire sentence as your oracle. It is permissible to interpret the sentence in its context, using what comes just before or after it to illuminate its application to your question.

Sometimes the text selected will be so obscure or inconsequential that you can make nothing useful out of it. When this happens, you should perform the divination a second time and use the second response.

Resist the urge to do this divination more than twice for any question, because the responses will quickly devolve into meaningless chaos. It is best to accept the initial text you receive unless it is completely meaningless. Bear in mind that sometimes the text will appear to lack meaning at the time you receive it, but later events will illuminate its meaning.

To end the exercise, close the book and press it to your chest as you take several silent breaths with your mind relaxed and empty.

Exercise 7.10: To Call the Four Winds

This exercise invokes the cleansing, purifying, and invigorating power of the four winds, which are spirits of the air associated with the four corners of the world.

Adopt the standing posture facing east with arms at your sides. Look straight ahead at the unseen distance horizon, ignoring what is in your field of view. Take a few silent breaths to calm and focus your thoughts.

Shift to an invoking posture by raising your arms above your head so that they form a V shape, and visualize yourself standing among the wildflowers of a mountain meadow. In front of you rises a blue mountain, and above it gather dark rain clouds. A warm but damp breeze blows down from the mountain against your face, carrying with it a fine mist of rain. It is scented with wildflowers. The breeze penetrates through you and cleanses your body, blowing away any trace of fatigue or weakness from your muscles. Feel it tingling in your arms and legs. Speak these words:

The east wind blows across the land; my legs are strong by which I stand.
Hail to thee, Eurus, spirit of the moist wind of the east.

Lower your arms and resume the standing posture, then rotate your body in a sunwise direction until you face the west. Take a few silent breaths to calm your mind. Gaze westward at the distant horizon.

Transition into the invoking posture, and visualize yourself standing in the sea grass on a sandy beach, looking out to sea. On the distant horizon, you can distinguish the white sail of a ship. Around and above its mast wheel white gulls. A gentle, cool breeze blows in your face, carrying with it the clean scent of the sea. It passes through you, strengthening your senses of vision and hearing. Speak these words:

The west wind blows across the sea; my eyes are clear by which I see.
Hail to thee, Zephyrus, spirit of the mild wind of the west.

Lower your arms in the standing posture and rotate your body in a sunwise direction until you face south. Pause to take a few silent breaths while looking straight ahead at the unseen horizon. Raise your arms to the south in the invoking posture.

Visualize a wildfire burning across a plane covered with dry brown grass and scrub trees. A hot wind fans the flames and sends the white smoke swirling and rolling forward. Smell the smoke from the burning. Waves of heat rise above the flames and make the air shimmer and dance. This hot wind passes through your body, but it does not cause discomfort. It purges your mind of all doubt or despair, driving away lethargy and leaving your thoughts sharp and clear. Speak these words:

The south wind blows across the flames; my thoughts are quick, my words the same.
Hail to thee, Notus, spirit of the hot wind of the south.

Lower your arms and assume the standing posture. Rotate your body sunwise to face the north, then take a few silent breaths. Direct your gaze forward at the level of the horizon, looking through the walls or other obstructions before you as though they were transparent. Raise your arms in invocation and elevate your gaze.

Visualize a barren landscape of black rock, ice, and blowing snow. The distant details are lost in the snow that swirls down on the wind. Feel the chill blast pass through your body. The cold air soothes any aches and pains you may have, as well as driving out fever and the heat of infection. Speak these words:

The north wind blows across the snow; no pain or illness do I know.
Hail to thee, Boreas, spirit of the cold wind of the north.

Lower your arms in the standing posture and rotate your body in a sunwise direction to face east, returning to your starting position.

Bring your feet together, close your hands into fists, cross them over your chest at the wrists, and shut your eyes. Hold this closing posture for a minute while you contemplate the four directions and the four winds around you—moist Eurus in front, mild

Zephyrus behind, hot Notus on your right side, and cold Boreas on your left side.

Then mentally release the spirits of the four winds as you turn your thoughts away from them.

Open your eyes, shift to a relaxed standing posture with arms at your sides, and take a few silent breaths to end the exercise.

REALIZATION

Realization is the fulfillment of your magic purpose. It is twofold and exists on two levels at the same time. It is the outward, tangible realization of the ritual purpose, but it is also an inward conviction and assurance that the magic has been successful. Not that it might be successful or will be successful, but that it *has been successful*. There is no "try" in magic. When you complete your ritual, it has either worked or not worked. If it has worked, you will experience an intuition of its working.

Realization on the inner plane may also be subdivided into two levels. You feel that the ritual has already succeeded, but you simultaneously hold your mind in such a state that it causes that fulfillment to occur. The fulfillment of the ritual is never forced—it cannot be forced—it is simply understood to exist, and this understanding brings it about.

A KIND OF MENTAL JUJITSU

This is the most difficult part of working magic, and also the hardest to explain to others, because the state your mind is in during realization, as I have called this aspect of the ritual process, has to be experienced to be fully comprehended. It involves a trick of the mind, a kind of mental jujitsu.

Realization does not entail willing the fulfillment of the purpose. That is the exact opposite of what we seek to achieve. When you will the achievement of a thing, it is the same as stating that you have not yet achieved it. It's like saying in the incantation, "I want to be a better person." As noted earlier, when you want something, it means you don't have it.

In ritual realization, we make ourselves aware that the ritual purpose has been fulfilled and hold this awareness in our minds, but we hold it there with no tension or desire for result. There cannot be the slightest degree of wishfulness or wanting or hoping. You must simply know below the level of words without actually thinking about it that your ritual purpose, as articulated in the incantation and expressed by dramatization, has been fulfilled. There must be a sense of quiet assurance that the thing is done, that it has been achieved, but it is important that this thought never be explicitly formed in your mind. There must be no trace of desire attached to it. It is simply an awareness that your work is done.

It is a very curious sensation that can only be fully understood by those who have experienced it firsthand. The surface of your mind must be held empty, but in your deep mind, you must have a calm conviction that amounts to a certainty that your purpose has been fulfilled. If there is any doubt, any worry, any mental activity concerning the work you have just performed, its realization will be frustrated. You must know that the ritual has been a success without ever thinking about its success.

A useful way to understand realization of purpose is to consider an archer who looses an arrow from his bow at a target. The target is the purpose you strive to achieve. The arrow is your will.

The bow focuses your will and concentrates its power when it is slowly drawn. The act of drawing the bow and aiming the arrow is the ritual enactment of your purpose. The release of the string that sends your arrow of will on its way is the realization. It is a moment of intense release, followed by a relaxation of tension and a softening of concentration. Once the arrow is loosed from the bow, it flies without the need for you to focus your mind upon it.

LASSITUDE OF REALIZATION

Ritual realization carries with it a physical lassitude or relaxation of the muscles throughout the entire body, which will bring about a sleepy condition. This may be so strong that you actually fall asleep shortly after completing the ritual. This is a good thing and a sign of success. The correct release of ritual purpose probably triggers the corresponding release of an endorphin in the brain that causes this pleasant lassitude, but so far as I am aware, no one has ever even attempted to identify which substance may be involved. You will know it when you feel it.

The lassitude that accompanies this mental duality is similar to the lassitude that follows immediately after sexual orgasm. In these few moments, the mind is blank, the body completely relaxed. It is not coincidental that some forms of magic following the left-hand path, as it is called, use the physical release of sexual orgasm to enable fulfillment of the ritual purpose. The act of orgasm provokes an intense focus of the will. It is followed by a release of care and the complete emptiness of mind that must occur if the ritual purpose is to be realized.

It is not necessary to use sexual energy when working magic. It is a crutch that skilled magicians do not need. Neither does a magician require the letting of blood or the sacrifice of an animal, although both acts have been used since ancient times to heighten emotional energy, focus it, and then release it like an arrow from a bow. When you have trained your powers of visualization and the concentration of your will and accompanied them with appropriate dramatic actions and incantations, the realization of your ritual purpose will occur without the need to spill either semen or blood.

STATEMENT OF REALIZATION

It can be useful at the end of a ritual to state in a deliberate way that the purpose for which you conducted it has been accomplished. This overt statement of realization is not absolutely necessary, but it helps terminate the working in your mind. For example, you might state aloud, "It is fulfilled" or "It is accomplished." If you wish to be even more explicit, you might describe the purpose of the working. For example, suppose you did magic to cause a certain person to visit you. Then you might state at the end of the ritual, "This ritual to summon John Smith is realized."

As you state aloud the realization, you release all desire to achieve the ritual purpose. It is the loosing of the arrow from the bow. All tension, both mental and physical, is released from you, and you then enjoy the lassitude that comes from the relaxing of effort for several minutes before you turn your thoughts to more mundane interests.

Following are some simple exercises that will allow you to practice this release of tension. They are designed to teach you how to realize your ritual purpose and should be regarded as examples. The most effective rituals are always those you create for the purpose at hand, and the most potent incantations are always those you yourself compose.

EXERCISES FOR CHAPTER 8

Exercise 8.1: Projecting a Thought

Set a photograph of someone you know well and will see in the near future upright on the table in front of your chair and sit in the sitting posture before it with feet flat on the floor and hands on your knees. If you don't have a photograph, you can visualize the face of the person in your mind. Take a few silent breaths to focus your intention. Look at the image of the person in the photograph. If you have no photograph, imagine the face of the person you wish to contact.

Concentrate upon the image of the face and project the force of your will outward, through the image to the actual person, as though the image were a psychic doorway. When you feel that you've made contact with that person, project to them a simple sentence. It should be something they might think of themselves, something that makes sense, such as, "It is a perfect day for the beach." Only project this if it actually is a perfect day for the beach. Or you might project, "I have a craving for pizza."

Look at the face in the photograph and use your will to project the words of the sentence. Project these words over and over to the person, and visualize the subject of the statement you are projecting. In the first example, it would be the image of a sunny, sandy beach, and in the second example, it would be a pizza in a pizza box.

When you have repeated the sentence a few dozen times, adopt the closing posture by making your hands into fists and crossing your forearms over your chest at the wrists. Close your eyes, and in a clear voice, speak the words "It is done."

Breathe several silent breaths, and while you do so, keep your mind empty of all thoughts or images. If you must think of something, think of the still, mirrorlike surface of a lake at twilight when the wind has died and there is no trace of a ripple on the water. But it is better to think of nothing.

Lower your hands, open your eyes, and resume the sitting posture. End the exercise by taking several silent breaths, then get up from the chair and go about your normal routine of activity. If thoughts of the ritual you have just performed threaten to creep into your mind, gently and without emotion turn them away. Simply forget about the ritual as you would forget about any incident of the day that has no importance.

If the person you focused your thoughts upon later tells you that they were thinking of you or makes a reference to whatever sentence you projected, you can call the exercise a success. They might mention that they thought it was a lovely day for the beach or felt a sudden craving for pizza, for example. Even if you get no confirmation that your projection was effective, the practice itself is useful for developing your skills in working magic.

Exercise 8.2: Projecting a Touch

This is something you may have done without even realizing it, or you may yourself have been the subject of such an event. When you find yourself among other people in a crowd, such as a schoolroom, a park, or a movie theater, choose a person at random who has his or her face turned away from you.

Unobtrusively place your left hand over your chest and point your right hand with your palm turned downward at the person you have selected. Make this projecting posture as discrete and understated as you need to make it to avoid the notice of those around you. It can be done standing or sitting.

Focus your attention on the back of the neck of your subject. Mentally extend the astral double of your right hand outward as though your right arm were elastic. You do not need to extend or even move your physical hand—project the astral double of the hand toward the person with the force of your will.

Keep your will focused on maintaining an astral link between your physical hand and your extended astral hand. Actually feel your astral hand as though it were your physical hand. You can draw vitality from inside your body to make this astral hand more tangible. Pull the energy from your heart-center into your left hand and send it looping up your left arm, across your shoulders, and down your right arm to extend your astral right hand.

Hold your astral hand close behind the person's neck and spread your fingers. Reach forward and gently grab the person by the back of the neck. It is helpful to move your physical fingers in the same way you move the fingers of your projected astral hand when you make this grabbing motion. As you do this, under your breath, speak the word "So!" in an emphatic way—or if you are too near others to speak without being noticed, speak it only inside your own mind.

As often as not, the person you perform this projection on will flinch, quickly turn their head, or reach up and rub their neck where you touched them astrally. They may even look directly at you. If so, do not meet their eyes but pretend that you have not noticed their attention on you.

Relax your will and allow your astral hand to draw back into your physical hand. Relax your body if you have tensed your muscles, and clear your mind. Take a few silent breaths to end the exercise.

There are numerous possible variations. You can use your projected astral hand to tickle someone's ear, ruffle their hair, or pat them on the shoulder.

You should refrain from malicious actions, as they tend to generate malicious reactions on the subconscious level. For example, if you astrally slap someone in the face, they may not consciously know what you have done, but they may suddenly feel a strong dislike for you without knowing why. It may even lead later to a physical confrontation. Be gentle, and be mentally detached. Remember, it is only an exercise to develop your skills.

Exercise 8.3: Astral Basin

Stand facing the east in the standing posture, and take a few silent breaths to calm your thoughts and prepare yourself. You may close your eyes if it aids your concentration, but you should also practice disregarding your physical surroundings with your eyes open to concentrate only on the astral forms with which you are working. You must learn to see with your inner sight even when your eyes are open.

Extend both hands before you, cupped palms upward with the little fingers touching, so that the palms form a kind of bowl. Visualize a large crystal basin resting on your hands. It is perfectly transparent and smooth.

When you have established the image of the basin in your thoughts, mentally extend your awareness upward above your hands into the heavens. Visualize a silvery stream of astral water falling straight downward into the basin. It is like the stream of water that runs from a partly opened tap. Actually try to see this thin silver stream descend into the crystal basin.

As the basin slowly fills with astral water, it becomes heavier and heavier. You must use more concentration to hold it out in front of you. Despite all the effort of your will, the weight of the water soon becomes so heavy that the basin begins to force your hands downward.

Struggle with the full effort of your will to continue to hold it, but when you feel that you can no longer support the basin, suddenly withdraw your mind from it so that it ceases to exist. Simultaneously, as you pull away your mind, speak the word "Done!" in an emphatic way and separate your cupped palms, turning them downward. Visualize the silvery astral water that was in the vanished basin suddenly drop to the floor with a great splash, and soak through the floor into the ground beneath.

Resume the standing posture and take a few silent breaths to relax. Turn your mind completely away from what you have just done and go about your day.

Exercise 8.4: Making Rain

The success of this exercise depends not only on your abilities to visualize and to focus your will but also on meteorological conditions. It can provoke a sudden cloudburst if conditions are right. Do not worry so much about the result, but concentrate on performing the exercise correctly.

Adopt the standing posture in the open air and look up at the sky. Visualize clouds gathering and slowly darkening from white to gray. Imagine their bellies fat with rain that is about to fall from them.

Raise your hands in the invoking posture to recite the following incantation:

Clouds do form and gather all.
Ere rise of dawn the rain will fall.

As you speak these words, turn your hands over so that your palms are downward, and extend your arms forward in front of you. Flutter your fingers as though shaking water droplets from their tips. Visualize drops of water falling from your fingertips.

Cross your forearms in front of your chest with your fists clenched, your eyes shut. In an emphatic tone, say, "It is fulfilled." It is not necessary to speak loudly. The words of realization can be any words you choose, provided they are simple, positive, and emphatic. As you state them, hold the emotional conviction in your mind for an instant that the work has been successfully fulfilled, then empty yourself of all thought, expectation, or desire for result.

Resume a relaxed standing posture with arms at your sides. Draw several silent breaths to clear your mind and end the exercise.

Exercise 8.5: To Provoke a Decision

When you wish to cause someone to come to a decision on a question they are pondering, you can help them by giving them a psychic nudge.

Begin in the standing posture and take a few silent breaths to relax and focus. If possible, stand facing the direction where you know that person is located. If you do not know where the person is, face the east.

Visualize the face of the indecisive individual as though looking at them through a window. Concentrate strongly on the person, while holding the question they cannot make up their mind about in your thoughts.

Recite the following incantation, and as you speak, project the meaning of the words strongly into the mind of the person you are visualizing.

Back and forth, up and down,
Yes and no, round and round,
Will or won't, do or don't,
Hound and hare will run about,
Now the matter once in doubt,
Decide!

When you reach the final word, step forward with your right foot and throw your hands forward forcefully as you project between them a bolt of psychic force at the person who is your target.

Immediately step back. Cross your forearms at the wrists in front of your chest with your fists closed, and shut your eyes. Release the tension within you and hold your mind empty for a minute or so. Avoid thinking of the person or the exercise you have just completed. Be aware with a quiet conviction that the question has already been resolved, but do not actually think about the question.

Shift into the standing posture and draw a few silent breaths to end the exercise.

Exercise 8.6: To Stop Bleeding

Magic has been used to stop the bleeding of wounds for thousands of years. This was a useful skill in past centuries for women who experienced a heavy monthly flow and wished to reduce its volume and duration. It was also used in emergency situations to reduce the flow of blood from cuts, such as those that occurred accidentally while hunting or in conflict on the battlefield.

Today we have paramedics, ambulances, and emergency wards in hospitals to handle such situations. Modern medicine, although mundane, is reliable in treating wounds and should always be the first resort in an emergency. But where no medical aid exists, this ancient remedy may be useful in slowing the loss of blood from a wound.

Lay your right hand over the area of bleeding, whether it be on your own body or the body of another person, and press your left hand to your chest. A woman who wishes to reduce her menstrual flow should place her right hand over her lower belly where her womb is located and her left hand over her heart. Visualize a mouth with tightly compressed lips, so that the lips are little more than pale, bloodless lines. Speak this incantation:

Red mouth sings a scarlet song.
Close its lips and stop its tongue.

Draw in your lips and press them strongly together. Hold them this way for a dozen seconds or so while continuing to visualize the sealed mouth in your mind.

Speak the realization "It is done!" in an emphatic way, and know in your own mind and heart that the bleeding has indeed stopped. You must know this with complete, perfect assurance in which there is no trace of doubt, without ever actually thinking it.

Exercise 8.7: To Pass Unnoticed

Invisibility is the art of not being noticed. You can't make your physical body cease to reflect light into the eyes of other human beings, but you can make others less aware of your presence, and when this is carried to its extreme, it is the same as making yourself invisible. They will not notice or care that you are present, will not talk to you or look at you, and will not remember at a later time that you were present.

The effect can be quite startling, as I myself discovered the first time I used invisibility magic. It is somewhat like moving through a dream. There are people around you, but they don't look at you. They still know you are there, in a way, because they don't bump into you, but you make no impression on their minds.

Begin in the standing posture facing the north, which is the quarter of darkness and shadow. Take a few silent breaths to relax and focus.

Visualize seeing yourself in a mirror, as if you were standing in your bathroom looking at yourself in the mirror of the medicine cabinet. Will your visualized reflection to become paler and begin to fade away. Make it gradually more transparent. As you watch it fade from view, speak the following incantation:

As a shadow lost in night
Fades to nothing in the light,
Fading, fading on the air,
Gone is one who wasn't there.

When your reflected image is almost invisible, speak the words, "Going, going, going, gone!" Close your eyes and empty your mind of thoughts and emotions. Do not think about what you have just done—detach yourself from it emotionally.

Open your eyes and take a few calming silent breaths to end the exercise.

The effect of the working will last for several hours, but it should be performed shortly before you go to the place where you wish to pass unnoticed. If you happen to encounter someone who knows you well or who is close to you, they may see you, but strangers will pay you little or no attention.

Exercise 8.8: Protection from Danger

When you are aware of a danger that threatens you in some way in the future and you can gain no protection from the police or other more conventional sources of aid, this exercise may help ward it off.

Begin in the standing posture facing the source of the danger if you know it and compose your mind by taking a few silent breaths. If you don't know where the danger is coming from, face the east and gaze at the distant unseen horizon.

Press the palms of your hands together in front of your breast in a gesture of prayer, and speak the following incantation of protection:

No hurt from wind or wave or fire,
Stone or steel or weapon dire,
Man or woman eld or child,
Beast or creature tame or wild,
Nor any threat from friend or foe,
Nor any danger where I go,
Shall harm a hair upon my head
On the day this charm is said.
By angels high and devils low,
By God in heaven, it is so!

As you say with emphasis the final words "it is so!," step back with your right foot and lean back slightly. Push your hands out in front of you at the level of your shoulders with the palms forward.

Hold this position for a few moments as you visualize a transparent wall between yourself and the danger that you believe threatens you. It is like a wall of diamond that cannot be broken by any force, device, creature, or spirit, extending endlessly upward, downward, and on either side. It wards off the danger and turns it harmlessly away. When needed, this astral wall will interpose itself between you and the danger that threatens.

Step forward with your right foot and assume the standing posture with arms at your sides. Take a few silent breaths to relax and end the exercise.

Exercise 8.9: Change Bad Luck to Good

Sometimes it requires only a very small action to change bad luck into good luck. Gamblers are conscious of this truth, but it applies in all areas of life. Luck is a kind of balance, and at times the balance needs to be adjusted.

Begin in a standing posture facing east. Relax and take a few silent breaths to prepare.

Position your left hand, palm downward, above your right hand, palm upward, in front of your solar plexus and press your palms together. Slowly separate your palms by about four inches and visualize a dark crystal sphere between them. Feel the top and bottom of the sphere touch the centers of your palms. It is filled with swirling shadows. This is your bad luck. See it churn inside the sphere like black thunderclouds. Speak the following incantation:

As night turneth into day
And winter into spring,
So the turning of my hands
Good luck to me doth bring.

Draw in a deep breath through your nose to fill your lungs, and release it slowly and audibly with a hissing sound between your lips. As you release the breath, rotate your palms with the transparent sphere held between them so that your right palm is now above your left palm. This is done by pivoting your hands at the wrists. While doing so, visualize the sphere becoming clear and filling with a bright blue-white light that is like starlight. Hold this shining bright sphere between your hands for a few seconds. It is filled with your good luck.

Slap your palms sharply together to absorb this light into your body, and as you do so, speak the single word "Change!"

Lower your arms into the standing posture and take a few silent breaths to end the exercise.

Exercise 8.10: Opening the Way

This exercise will remove obstacles and barriers that prevent you from advancing your purpose. Use it when you wish to do something but find yourself frustrated and unable to move forward.

Adopt a standing posture facing the direction of your obstacle if you know its location—otherwise, face the east. Take a few silent breaths.

Shift into a posture of prayer with your hands pressed together in front of your breast, and speak the following incantation:

Frost will crack the hardest rock,
An axe will split the toughest tree,
A key unbinds the strongest lock,
A river always finds the sea;
The way is open where I walk,
No bar or bolt can hinder me.

Visualize double doors in front of you that are sheathed in shining gold. Imagine your purpose on the other side of those doors. Extend your hands forward with their backs touching, then spread them wide as though opening the two sides of a curtain. As you make this opening motion, visualize the imagined doors part in the middle and swing outward, away from you, to open your path forward to your purpose. Visualize bright sunlight spilling upon you through the opening doors. Speak these words of realization with emphatic force: "The way is opened!"

Resume the standing posture and breathe a few silent breaths to relax your mind and end the exercise.

THE AURA

The magic circle has for many centuries been considered an essential part of Western ritual magic. In old woodcuts, you will see magicians standing inside a circle that is drawn or painted on the floor while summoning demons. Witches were sometimes depicted dancing outdoors in a ring back-to-back with their arms linked. Their joined bodies formed the magic circle of their art.

At the most basic symbolic level, a magic circle represents the expanded boundary of the magician who stands within it. The circle defines the sphere of control, the place where the magician's will rules and the magician's commands are obeyed. The circle is the expanded self. Within the circle there is reason and order, but outside the circle there is misrule and chaos.

This is how the astrologer Ebenezer Sibly explained the purpose of the magic circle in his monumental work, *A New And Complete Illustration of the Celestial Science of Astrology*, the first part of which was published in 1784:

> The reasons assigned by magicians and others for the institution and use of circles, is, that so much ground being

> blessed and consecrated by such holy words and ceremonies as they make use of in forming it, hath a secret force to expel all evil spirits from the bounds thereof; and, being sprinkled with pure sanctified water, the ground is purified from all uncleanness; besides, the holy name of God being written over every part of it, its force becomes so powerful, that no evil spirit hath ability to break through it, or to get at the magician or his companion, by reason of the antipathy in nature they bear to these sacred names. . . . The circle therefore, according to this account of it, is the principal fort and shield of the magician, from which he is not, at the peril of his life, to depart, till he has completely dismissed the spirit, particularly if he be of a fiery or infernal nature.[10]

Traditionally, when working outdoors, the magic circle was scratched into the ground with a sharp instrument such as a knife or sword or marked by trailing a thin line of salt, chalk dust, or sand over the ground. Sometimes strips of animal skin were pinned to the ground with nails or thorns to make the circle. When magic was worked indoors, a temporary circle was drawn on the floor using a stick of charcoal or chalk, or a more permanent circle was painted on the floor. It was often an elaborate construction of two or more concentric rings between which were inscribed occult symbols and names of power.

It is important that you understand the core concept of the magic circle. It's not just a line drawn on the floor. It is what divides the limited from the limitless, the inside from the outside, the known and controlled from the unknown and chaotic. What

---

10. Ebenezer Sibly, *A New and Complete Illustration of the Celestial Science of Astrology*, 13th ed. (London, 1826), 1103.

lies within the circle is discrete and has definite form and function. What lies beyond its limit is everything else that is unbounded.

A word is a kind of magic circle. For example, when you say the word *apple*, you draw a boundary in your mind around the concept of the red fruit that grows on a tree, and this boundary defines the shape of that concept. The boundary is how you understand what the word means. All other actual and potential words lie outside it.

I don't mean to belabor the point, but it has become evident to me over the years that most who work magic have no concept of what the magic circle actually is, what it does, or how it does it. The reason the magic circle was said in folklore to be impassable by demons is because it represents an absolute division of one place from another. What is outside does not touch in any way what is inside.

THE HUMAN AURA

The aura is a kind of magic circle. The concept of the aura, as it exists in modern magic, was popularized in 1903 by the Theosophist Charles Leadbeater in his book *Man Visible and Invisible*. Leadbeater was responsible for establishing the idea that an energy field surrounds the human body. Leadbeater taught that this energy field is usually invisible to the human eye, but psychics are sometimes able to perceive it.

He believed that this energy field changes shape and color depending on the health, emotions, and thoughts of the person from whom it emanates and that it is possible to psychically investigate the health of an individual by examining that person's aura. In the thirteenth chapter of his book, he gave a list of colors and forms that appear in the aura and associated them with various states of being. For example, he asserted that anger made the aura red, hatred and malice blackened it, sparkling golden stars indicated spiritual aspirations, and so on.[11]

Theosophy teaches that a human is made up of various levels of being. The lowest of these is the physical body itself. Interpenetrating this is the etheric double, a kind of subtle duplication of the physical body. More refined still is the astral body, and still more elevated in a spiritual sense is the mental body, above which is the causal body. All these bodies nest one inside the other like Russian nesting dolls, with the physical body at the center. Theosophists believe that each body can express itself to the visual perception of psychics as various aspects of the human aura.

This idea was simplified and mainlined to the modern esoteric community in 1977 by Christopher Hills in his book *Nuclear Evolution: Discovery of the Rainbow Body*. Hills wrote that surrounding our physical body are seven subtle bodies, which he assigned to the colors of the rainbow. You will encounter this paradigm frequently in images of the aura, which show the human body surrounded by seven layers colored the seven colors of the light spectrum that appear when light shines through a glass prism. The layer nearest the skin is shown as red, and the layer most distant is shown as violet.

We are not going to delve into the theoretical chromatic subtleties of the aura in this book because there is no need. However, we will use the aura as a magic circle in the following exercises, and it is necessary to at least touch on what many modern magicians believe to be the nature and composition of the aura.

The concept of the human aura, as a visible field or envelope that surrounds the body, goes back much further in history than

11. Charles W. Leadbeater, *Man Visible and Invisible: Examples of Different Types of Men as Seen by Means of Trained Clairvoyance*, 2nd ed. (London: Theosophical Publishing House, 1920), 80, 81, 85.

Leadbeater's book. We find it in the accounts of Christian, Buddhist, and Hindu writers of past centuries when they write about the halo, the nimbus, the glory, the mandorla, and the aureole seen around the bodies of saints and holy persons. All of these are different aspects of the human aura. The halo is light seen around the head, the aureole or mandorla is an oval of light around the entire body, and the nimbus is sometimes considered to be a combination of these two. They are all a single phenomenon that has been observed in various ways by countless thousands of individuals over a span of thousands of years.

SENSORY METAPHORS

In my opinion, the aura is not a field of physical energy around the human body, and it cannot be seen with the human eye. The aura is an interpretation or translation by the mind of something that is not visual into an apparent visual perception. You may have heard of people who hear colors or see sounds. This condition is called synesthesia and is recognized to exist by modern science.

The mind has the ability to create sense impressions without the input of the physical senses—to create a color when no color is seen by the eye, for example, based on a sound heard by the ear. But it can do much more than this. The human mind can change perceptions that are nonsensory into perceptions that appear to be sensory. In some of my other books, I have referred to these transmuted perceptions as sensory metaphors.

The mind does this because this type of translation is the only way our consciousness can be made aware of these nonsensory perceptions. The aura is the translation by the mind of a perception of something that cannot be seen, heard, touched, tasted, smelled, or perceived in any physical manner into what appears to be a visual envelope of energy surrounding the body.

What is true of the aura is true of the astral world in general. Our physical eyes cannot see astral forms. They are perceived with the mind, and the mind then translates them into visual impressions that we mistakenly think we are seeing with our physical eyes. If the mind did not translate its impression of the aura into some sensory metaphor that we are capable of understanding, we would never become consciously aware of it. In order to convey information to us that we would otherwise be unable to access, the deep mind tricks our consciousness into believing that we see the aura with our physical eyes.

Understand my meaning. I am not suggesting that the aura is unreal. It is a very real phenomenon that has been documented by countless witnesses over a span of thousands of years. However, it is not physical; it is not an energy field around the body that can be measured by machines, and it is not actually seen with the physical eyes. It is the translation by the mind of something that is real but beyond our physical senses into something we mistakenly assume we are seeing with our eyes. When we see the aura, it looks like a tangible envelope of light surrounding the body, but there is no actual light there. The perception of light is being created in our minds, based on something real that is intuited by the mind, but that we cannot sense in any physical way.

DESCRIPTIONS OF AURAS VARY

I do not believe it is important to delve into the complex structure of the aura that has been imagined and detailed by various Theosophists and writers on the occult, because accounts are so variable. One person sees the aura one way, another person sees it another way; one person sees one color, another sees another color; one person sees one pattern or form, another sees a different pattern or form. Most people who are not psychic see no aura at all throughout their entire lives—although auras are much easier to see around highly spiritual individuals than around average human beings and have been seen around such people even by those with no obvious psychic ability.

Accounts of auras are so variable because each person who sees an aura is actually perceiving in their mind, beyond the level of sense impressions, a translation of a nonsensory event. Each person's mind makes this translation in a slightly different way, although the overall impression of the aura is always that of a field of light surrounding the body or the head. For this reason, I think it is futile to try to pin down any complex system of layers or colors in the aura. What is perceived by one person will not be perceived in the same way by another person.

In this book, we will deal with the aura only as an astral envelope that is traditionally said to surround the body. It will be described in conventional terms. For the sake of simplicity, we will treat it as a transparent shell that can be shaped, contracted, or expanded by the power of the will.

THE AURIC SPHERE

You have no need to physically draw a circle around you when you work your magic. You can use the aura that always surrounds your body as your magic circle. In order to do this, the aura must be visualized clearly. In its normal resting state, the aura lies close to your skin. The distance usually varies, somewhere between less than an inch to several inches, depending on your energy level and state of mind. When you are full of vigor and feeling good, your aura expands slightly, and when you are exhausted or depressed, it contracts.

When a magic circle is needed in order to create a working space around you, one way you can create it is by expanding your aura beyond its normal extent so that it forms a sphere. It is convenient to expand this sphere to a diameter between nine and twelve feet. Smaller and it is difficult to work within; larger and it will extend beyond the walls of your practice room and be more difficult to visualize. Make it big enough that you can work within it without awkwardness.

While you are standing, this expanded auric sphere will extend a few feet above your head and below your feet, but its equator at the level of your navel will be four or five feet away from your torso on all sides. Think of it as a transparent ball that you stand inside. Because it is astral in nature, it extends through any physical object that may happen to be close to your body, such as the floor beneath your feet or the ceiling above your head. Physical substances cannot block astral forms.

Just as your skin is the limit of your physical body, your aura is the limit of your astral body. Within the sphere of your aura are the things you control and possess; beyond it lie those things you do not control or possess but with which you interact. Within the envelope of the aura is the microcosm, or lesser universe; beyond it lies the macrocosm, or greater universe. What divides the two is the boundary of your aura, your natural magic circle.

During astral travel, when the astral double is projected beyond the physical body, the aura stretches to link the physical body with the distant astral double. This stretched aura takes the form of what has been called the silver cord, an elastic link between the separated physical and astral bodies.

Do not be dismayed if you are unable to actually perceive the sensory metaphor of the aura around you while you are working with it. Not everybody is able to see the light of the aura. Some of us, myself included, can see auras only at certain times of heightened perception, or when the emotions of the bearer of the aura are strongly elevated. I seldom see colors of any kind. My brother once told me he could see the auras around other people easily, just by looking at them. You can work with the aura without ever actually seeing it, by relying on the power of visualization.

THE HEART-CENTER

It is possible to pass something into or out of a magic circle without breaking the circle. When this happens, the thing that was outside becomes part of what is inside, or the thing that was inside becomes part of what is outside. The gateway through any circle lies at the point of its center. This central point is the only way, esoterically speaking, into or out of a magic circle without dividing the circle, and a circle divided is no longer a circle.

Since all points within a circle are featureless, dimensionless, and identical, all points may be considered the central point. The center of anything is defined by your point of view. You are the center. You look outward in all directions at the greater universe. If you choose to regard a point outside your body as the center and view the world from that point, then it becomes, for you, the center.

In ancient times, most people regarded Earth as the center of the universe. This was natural, since the sphere of Earth corresponded with their own point of view. A consequence was the prevailing belief of the ancients that the sun, and indeed everything in the heavens, revolved around Earth. We see this even today in the geocentric charts of astrology. But with the dawn of the age of reason, scientists began to convince others to artificially project their point of view outside their own body, and from this projected viewpoint, it became possible to regard things other than Earth as the center. For example, it was possible to conceive the sun as the center of the solar system and to conceive Earth as revolving around it.

In magic, we usually adopt the ancient and more natural understanding that the center of everything is the point from which we regard the greater world around us. We are the center of our universe. However, we understand that we may mentally shift our point of view to anywhere in the universe, and when we do so, it becomes the center for us.

Philosophically and symbolically, the center of the human body is the heart. This is easy to demonstrate. Consider the popular expression "get to the heart of the matter." What does it mean? It means to get to the center of something. When you are in the "heart of the city," you are in the center of the city. The "heartland" is the land in the middle. When something is "heartfelt," it touches you to the core of your being. The "heartwood" of a tree is the wood at the center.

When you wish to move esoteric forces into and out of your body, you can do so by opening your heart-center, an esoteric center located in the middle of your chest. These forces are moved inward through this opened gateway into your heart-center from outside your aura, or outward from your heart-center to beyond your aura.

Forces, and even spiritual beings, can also be invoked or banished from other esoteric centers in your body, but at this stage in your study, we will focus only on the heart-center, which is the natural center of your body.

The heart-center is located in the middle of the chest roughly in the heart region but slightly below it and on the centerline of the body behind the sternum. It is behind and slightly above the nerve juncture known as the solar plexus, at the base of the sternum.

You should visualize this center as a perfect sphere of soft-white light that is approximately the size of a baseball. The energy of the sphere causes it to rotate in a counterclockwise direction about its vertical axis, when viewed from above, just as Earth rotates on its axis in a counterclockwise direction, when viewed from above the northern pole. The more energy contained within your heart-center, the more rapidly it will rotate. As you draw energy into it from outside the envelope of your aura, it spins more rapidly, and as you project energy out of it and beyond your aura, it spins more slowly.

In the following exercises, we will use the expanded aura as a magic circle and the heart-center as its gateway, through which esoteric forces may be drawn into the circle or expelled out from it.

EXERCISES FOR CHAPTER 9

Exercise 9.1: Sensing Your Aura

The aura of others appears as a visual impression, and if you have the gift of perceiving auras, you can examine your own aura by standing in front of a mirror, but your aura can also be sensed by touch.

Assume a standing posture facing east and take a few silent breaths to calm and focus your mind.

Close your eyes and direct your attention to the surface of your skin. Become aware of the skin covering your entire body. Your physical skin on the material plane corresponds with your aura on the astral plane. It encloses you and protects you from the intrusion of hostile microorganisms. It keeps what is inside in and what is outside out. In this sense, your skin is a magic circle.

Visualize in a tactile way the pressure of your aura upon your skin. This pressure is very light and easy to overlook, but when you concentrate on it, you will find that you can feel a soft pressure, like that of a very light breeze, that stirs the small hairs on your arms and legs. It can be helpful, in the beginning, to do this exercise naked, as this removes the distraction of the pressure from your clothing. Even if you cannot feel your aura surrounding your body, visualize the sensation of it lying lightly against your skin like an almost weightless, invisible blanket.

When you have held your focus on this sensation for several minutes, take a few silent breaths to empty your mind, and open your eyes to end the exercise.

Exercise 9.2: Visualizing Your Aura

Practice on a regular basis visualizing your aura around your body outside your clothing, several inches away from your skin.

Adopt the standing posture facing the east. As usual, relax and focus your thoughts with a few silent breaths.

Visualize the boundary of your aura as a pleasant, transparent violet color—that is, as blue with a hint of purple. It is a vibrant, alive color. At the same time you are visualizing it in your imagination, open your awareness to perceive the flashes of color that change and move over its surface. Spend about five minutes on this exercise.

It may be easier in the beginning to do the visualization with your eyes closed, but you should also practice visualizing in your mind while your eyes are open and focused on the unseen distant horizon. The trick of this is to hold your attention on the inner visualization and ignore completely the actual scene you are looking at with your eyes. See with your inner sight, and ignore your outer sight.

Relax your attention and take a few silent breaths to end the exercise.

Exercise 9.3: Visualizing Your Heart-Center

The heart-center and the aura are connected, in the sense that the expanded aura is the magic circle and the heart-center is the center of that circle. The heart-center can be made to serve the function of an altar—it becomes the focal point of ritual work, where the magic intention is actualized.

The point of view you adopt for this exercise is up to you. I suggest that you imagine yourself viewing the spinning sphere of your heart-center from behind your back, as if your back were transparent and you were standing behind your body, but you can also imagine yourself staring straight down upon the sphere of your heart-center from the viewpoint of your head. Where you choose to project your point of self is up to you.

Adopt a standing posture facing east, and take a few silent breaths to prepare. In the beginning of your practice, it may help to close your eyes.

Visualize a soft-white sphere floating in the middle of your hollow chest. It is around the size of a baseball or somewhat smaller. Imagine that this white sphere rotates counterclockwise on its vertical axis. Its spin corresponds in miniature to the rotation of Earth, which also turns on its axis counterclockwise, from the traditional perspective of the Northern Hemisphere. Try to also feel this sphere turning inside your chest. Feel its energy. It is like a dynamo, densely charged with vital force.

Hold this visualization for several minutes, then open your eyes and take a few silent breaths to end the exercise. You should also practice this visualization with your eyes open.

Exercise 9.4: Tinting Your Aura

This exercise may be done with your eyes open or closed, but you should practice doing it with eyes open once you gain some familiarity with it.

In this description of the exercise, the color is yellow, but you should vary the color you choose for your aura from one practice session to another. It is best to imagine only pure, bright colors. One approach is to work your way down through the spectrum from violet to red, choosing a different color of the rainbow each day for seven days, and then repeat the exercise in seven-day cycles. Visualize only a single color for each exercise, and strive to become aware of how this visualization affects your actual sensations, emotions, and thoughts.

Adopt a standing posture facing east, and take a few silent breaths to focus and prepare your mind.

Visualize your transparent aura surrounding your body. Imagine that it extends outward several inches away from your skin in this visualization—its actual extent will vary with your emotional state and vitality level. Begin by picturing it as colorless.

Visualize your aura slowly changing to a bright, transparent yellow. You can imagine looking at your body from the front or the back, whichever you prefer. See yourself standing surrounded by your aura, which has turned yellow as though it were a transparent balloon filled with a bright yellow gas.

Hold this visualization, and open your awareness to any perceptions that may arise from your aura. These may take the form of sensations on your skin, emotions, or brief flashes of thought.

When you have sustained a yellow tint in your auric envelope for several minutes, mentally allow it to fade once again to a clear transparency. Draw a few silent breaths and relax your mind to end the exercise.

Exercise 9.5: Expanding Your Aura

Adopt a standing posture facing east. Gaze straight ahead. Visualize your aura around your body. Without closing your eyes, raise your hands and touch them back-to-back in front of your chest, then slowly push forward and outward to the sides as though doing a breaststroke in swimming. Or you can imagine pushing open the sliding double doors of an elevator. As you extend your hands to either side, the palms turned outward, visualize in your imagination that you are pushing your aura wider from the inside with energy that radiates from the palms of your hands.

With your arms fully extended to the sides at shoulder level, palms turned outward, hold in your mind an image of your aura expanded into a perfect sphere around you, like a giant transparent soap bubble. Iridescent flashes of color may come and go across its stretched surface. It passes through the furniture near you and through the floor under your feet because it is astral, and physical objects cannot obstruct astral objects.

Hold the expanded aura for a minute or so, then slowly cross your forearms at the wrists in front of your chest, with your left wrist touching your chest, making your hands into fists as you do so. Close your eyes. When you contract your arms, visualize your aura shrinking back to its normal shape, like an inflated balloon from which the air is released. Remain in this posture for a minute with your mind empty, breathing normally.

Open your eyes and resume a relaxed standing posture with arms at your sides. Take a few silent breaths to end the exercise.

Exercise 9.6: Hardening the Aura

At times you may find yourself under a psychic influence that results in obsessive emotions of a destructive kind, such as fear or depression. You may even believe yourself to be the victim of an outright astral attack. One form of defense against this intrusion into your personal space is to harden your aura, making it resistant to penetration. This technique was taught by the Hermetic Order of the Golden Dawn.[12]

One way to harden the aura is by contracting it until it lies very close to your skin. You can set your aura to this state by a deliberate act of will.

To practice hardening the aura, face east with your arms at your sides in a standing posture. Take a few silent breaths to clear your mind.

Close your eyes. Visualize the aura surrounding your body, and at the same time, feel it on your skin. When you have a clear sense of your aura, cross your forearms over your chest at the wrists, your hands closed into fists. Use the power of your will to contract your aura nearer and nearer to your skin. Visualize it glowing with a brighter bluish tint in your imagination. Draw it inward until it becomes like a glowing astral second skin, then mentally fix it in this position by concentrating strongly on it. Speak the affirmative words "It is done."

Immediately turn your mind away from your aura. Open your eyes and relax your arms at your sides in the standing posture. Draw a few silent breaths to end the exercise.

---

12. Israel Regardie, *The Golden Dawn*. 6th ed. (St. Paul, MN: Llewellyn Publications, 1990), 88. See also Regardie, *The Middle Pillar*, 3rd ed. (St. Paul, MN: Llewellyn Publications, 1998), 211.

Keep in the back of your mind a quiet assurance that what you sought to achieve by contracting your aura has been accomplished. Don't say this to yourself or try to trick yourself into believing it. Don't even think about it—simply know it to be true without a trace of doubt.

After a time, which will vary from a few minutes to about an hour depending on the strength of your will, the aura will return to its natural state. If you wish to sustain a hardened aura, you must periodically perform this exercise to renew its tension when it begins to relax.

You should not try to keep your aura hardened for an extended period of time. It is not the natural condition of your aura, and if held this way for too long, it will unbalance and hinder the free circulation of esoteric energies in your body.

Exercise 9.7: Changing Aura Colors with Emotions

Adopt a standing posture facing east. Keep your eyes open and gaze straight ahead at the unseen distant horizon. Take a few silent breaths to relax.

Visualize in your mind your aura as a colorless, transparent envelope around your body. Imagine it slowly changing from colorless to a clear, bright blue, and as you do so, think of something that is pure and beautiful, such as a flower or the laughter of a child. Hold this blue color for a minute.

Visualize your aura changing to a deep red, and as you do so, think of something that makes you angry. See the color shift from blue to red as clearly as possible in your imagination. Hold the red color for a minute or so.

Calm your thoughts and imagine your aura changing to a bright transparent yellow. As you do this, keep your mind balanced and alert. Think of something that inspires you, such as a beautiful work of art, a great human achievement, or a famous landmark. Hold the yellow for a minute or so.

Finally, cause your aura to gradually shift from yellow back to bright blue as you think of a higher spiritual being you respect. It doesn't matter which spirit you focus on, as long as it is a spirit that is compassionate and good. Christians may wish to focus on Jesus, the Virgin Mary, one of the saints, or an archangel. Pagans might choose to focus on the Goddess or one of the noble pagan deities such as Balder or Isis.

Hold each of these colors for at least a minute before shifting to the next color, and try to actually see them in your mind rather than just picturing them.

To end the exercise, relax and take a few silent breaths.

Exercise 9.8: Mirror Meditation

Dim the lights and assume a standing posture in front of a full-length mirror, if you have access to one. If not, any large mirror will serve, such as a bathroom cabinet mirror. Gaze at your reflection and take a few silent breaths to calm your mind.

Visualize your aura in the mirror, surrounding your reflected image. Strive to see it as clearly as possible, as you would if you were someone with the developed psychic ability to see the auras of others. Take note of its shape, its size, and the colors that pass over its surface with each of your thoughts. Do this for several minutes.

Mentally project your point of view into your mirror image, and visualize that you are standing inside the mirror. See and feel yourself inside the mirror world as you gaze out at your physical body and the aura that surrounds it, as though you were gazing through a window. Look into your physical eyes from inside the mirror and hold the awareness of your visualization for a minute or two, before allowing your point of view to return into your physical body.

Relax and take a few silent breaths to end the exercise.

Exercise 9.9: Cleansing the Aura

Adopt a standing posture facing east, and breathe deeply a few silent breaths to clear and focus your mind.

Visualize your aura surrounding you as you think of a problem or worry that has been on your mind. See your negative feelings expressed in your aura. Muddy, dark colors such as clouds of brown or gray signify worry and depression, deep red indicates anger, and black expresses hatred. The specific shades, tints, and textures seen will vary from person to person, but in general these color correspondences will occur.

Spread your arms wide at shoulder level, and visualize a cascade of white light falling from the heavens over the surface of your aura. Watch in your mind this celestial rain of light as it cleanses your aura of its dark and muddy colors. When your aura is washed to a clear, transparent blue, allow your negative thoughts and emotions to be swept away with the rain of light and carried into the ground below you.

Lower your arms to resume the standing posture, and take a few silent breaths to end the exercise.

Exercise 9.10: Extending the Aura

Your aura can never be divided, but it can be shaped and extended. This is sometimes useful when you wish to take an object, a person, or even a place into your auric envelope for healing or protection. In this exercise, we will absorb a wooden kitchen chair into our aura, but any other simple object will serve just as well.

Adopt a standing posture in front of the chair, and draw a few silent breaths to calm and focus your mind.

Expand your aura into a sphere as you did in exercise 5 of this chapter (page 157), and hold it fully expanded for a minute or so.

Slowly bring your widespread arms forward with your palms turned toward the front, as though pushing at something in front of you. At the same time, visualize the wall of your auric sphere bulge away from you in response to the energy flowing out from your palms.

Visualize a counterclockwise vortex form in the wall of your aura in front of you, and enlarge this turning spiral. In this way, you deliberately open a portal in your auric envelope that allows you to take something into your expanded aura. If you did not consciously form this vortex, it would form automatically as you extended your aura around the chair with a deliberate act of will, but it is useful to be aware that you are opening your aura to accept something into it.

Continue expanding the front of your auric sphere until it bulges like a transparent balloon around the chair. When the chair is inside your aura, shrink the vortex portal to a point and allow it to vanish.

You can shape this bulge in your aura into a globe that is connected with the main part of your aura by only a narrow channel. The silver cord that is said by psychics to connect a projected astral body with its physical body is an example of this extended auric channel, which is infinitely elastic. It is a sensory metaphor, not a physical conduit, so it can be stretched as far as is needed.

After holding the bulge in the front of your aura around the chair for a minute or two, once again create a vortex in its forward wall and draw the bulge back to eject the chair. Close the vortex and allow your aura to return to a sphere as you spread your arms wide to the sides once again.

Make a mental connection between your hands and the sides of your aura, and draw your arms inward, crossing them in front of your chest with your hands closed into fists. As you do so, contract your aura to its normal shape near your skin. Shut your eyes and contemplate your natural aura around your body for a minute or so.

Open your eyes, shift into a standing posture with your arms at your sides, and take a few silent breaths to end the exercise.

SCRYING

Scrying is the psychic perception of hidden or distant things. It functions in the past, present, or future, not only in the material world but also in the astral realm of spirits. According to the *Oxford English Dictionary*, the term *scry* derives from *descry*—to see or perceive.[13] Usually it is used in connection with crystal gazing, but scrying is not limited to sight.

Scrying is a predominantly passive form of magic. The mind of the scryer opens itself to psychic sensory impressions, which commonly present themselves as sights or sounds because these are the senses we most depend on, but these impressions can also come as scents, feelings of touch, or even tastes—for example, scrying an infernal demon might produce a smell of burning sulfur or a taste of excrement in the mouth.

Magicians have always relied on scrying to gain information and communications from the astral world. Shamans dancing around campfires ten thousand years ago scried visions of the hunt and painted them on cave walls with red ochre. The prophecies of

13. *Oxford English Dictionary*, compact ed. (1971), under "scry."

the Old Testament were all scried, either deliberately or involuntarily. The druid Merlin, teacher of Arthur Pendragon, was famed in later centuries for his skill in crystal scrying.

In ancient times, scrying was considered a necessary skill for working spirit magic. Egyptian, Greek, and Jewish magicians would employ young children, usually boys, as their scryers, because children have a natural gift of second sight. These magicians would rely on the eyes and ears of the boys during ritual evocations. It was the children's job to describe what spirits called forth into the ritual chamber were doing and to repeat the words spoken by the spirits when the magicians questioned them. These magicians could not themselves see or hear the spirits they conjured up and commanded.

It may come as a surprise, in these days of spirit mediums and channelers behind every bush, but the magicians of ancient times were almost never passive psychics. To judge by the Jewish, Egyptian, and Arab grimoires that have come down to us from the early centuries of the present era, it was regarded as normal that a magician would employ another person to see and hear spirits summoned during rituals.

Of course, it is much more convenient when doing spirit magic to be able to perceive the responses of spirits directly, without the need for a medium. Even those who never intend to summon spirits will find the ability to scry useful in their magic work. Scrying can reveal the location of lost or hidden items. It can yield information about past or distant events. It can even reveal the future.

Attempting to work magic without some scrying ability is like trying to run with a bad knee. It can be done, after a fashion, but how much better the result is if the magician can scry, at least on some basic level. The exercises at the end of this chapter are designed to develop your latent scrying ability.

Scrying is a skill, like any other. Regular practice will improve your results. Scrying is also a natural talent that some have to a greater degree than others. Just as there are people who are tone deaf and cannot sing and people who have two left feet and cannot dance, so are there people with no scrying ability. But most of us have at least some inherent gift for seership on some level, using one scrying method or another. You should experiment with various techniques to find the best one for you.

WHO MAKE THE BEST SEERS

It was thought in past generations that men make the best seers. All the great prophets of the Old Testament were men, and Merlin, who was reputed to be the greatest scryer of all time, was a man. However, in my personal experience, I have found this not to be true. I have found that women are more often naturally gifted with passive psychic abilities. The main point I wish to make is that anyone can scry. Nor is there any age barrier. Young children are naturally receptive to psychic influences, but scryers can be any age or gender.

Celts have been particularly famed in the past for their ability to scry, which they sometimes refer to as the second sight. The Irish, the Scots, and the Welsh are all reputed to be uncommonly sensitive to astral impressions. I'm one-quarter Welsh on my father's side, and I sometimes wonder how much this part of my heritage has influenced my own ability to scry. The Romani tribes also gained a reputation for passive psychic abilities. Even if you don't fall into one of these special groups, there is no reason to be discouraged—every nation has its seers.

Another factor said to influence scrying ability is family heritage. The gift of seership runs in families, although it may skip generations. My grandfather, on my mother's side, was a talented crystal gazer and tea-leaf reader. My mother also had second sight, although she never tried to develop her gift in a systematic way, and my brother has some scrying ability—he can see auras, for example. You should take note whether any member of your family has exhibited psychic gifts. It may indicate that you have a similar talent latent within you.

SIGHT AND SOUND SCRYING

Scrying is traditionally linked to the powers of the moon and to the things occultly associated with the moon. Most forms of sight-crying rely on lunar substances such as water, glass, crystal, silver, and mirrors. The scryer gazes into a reflective or shiny surface with a receptive mind, and images arise.

Aura reading is a type of sight scrying in which the shape and colors of the occult energy envelope that surrounds the human body are perceived and interpreted as indicators of physical, emotional, and mental states. We've already examined the nature of the aura—here, we will practice gaining a first perception of it.

Sound scrying commonly relies on background noise as a matrix in which to hear psychic sounds and voices. The whisper or moan of the wind in the trees, the babble of a brook, road noise when driving in a car, the rumble of a hot-air furnace or an air conditioner—these are the kinds of low-level background sounds that promote sound-scrying. White noise is not particularly good for sound scrying because it is too uniform. The best kind of background noise is a regular rumble, hiss, or gurgle that has mixed into it slight variations of sound. The passive mind finds it easy to use these kinds of background noises as the basis upon which to build psychic sound impressions.

How does sound scrying work? All day long your mind is filled with voices of spirits speaking to each other, or talking to you, but you don't hear them because an automatic active agency of your mind filters them out so that you can think, read, and concentrate on daily activities.

This automatic filter works the same way when your hearing is shut off while you sleep. Many times I have noticed that when I wake up, I will lie for several seconds before my hearing suddenly cuts in, and I can hear the background noises in my house. Until my hearing abruptly engages itself, there is complete silence, even though I am fully awake. This filter allows important sounds, such as alarms, to get through while you are sleeping, but it shuts off distracting noises.

Cats have this ability to an even greater degree than we do. A cat automatically shuts out sounds that are of no interest to it, while still being able to hear sounds that are important to it. You've probably seen cats lying unconcerned in the noisiest environments, seemingly deaf to the din, but the instant a sound comes that interests the cat, its ears prick up and it darts off to investigate.

The voices of spirits constantly talking in our heads would drive us insane if we did not have an inherent filter to suppress them. When we sound scry, we are tricking this filter and allowing a portion of those voices to reach our conscious awareness. Often the result is an incomprehensible babble, but at times a single voice or scraps of a conversation will come through more strongly than the babbling background voices.

Hearing ghost voices over the radio is another form of sound scrying. This is done by scanning across the radio dial and listening to the bursts of static between stations and the brief words or parts of words that come through from radio programs. You can buy digital devices called ghost boxes to make this practice easier. My wife, Jenny, spent a year studying this form of electronic sound scrying and got excellent results from it. She discusses it in her book *Spiritual Alchemy* (Llewellyn, 2016).

SCRYING BY TOUCH

Sight and sound are the two most useful senses for scrying because they carry the most information, but it is also possible to scry by touch. When a spirit is present, perceptive individuals often sense it on their skin in the form of a slight breeze or a coolness. Some haunted houses have persistent cold spots that are perceptible to psychics. The chill of a spirit's touch is distinct and very real, even though it is a sensory metaphor. If you feel it, you will know—you won't need to wonder whether you felt it or didn't feel it.

The touch of spirits is usually cool, but it is not unpleasant. I have an uncommon sensitivity to touch impressions and have felt the touch of many spirits, so I can describe them firsthand. In addition to coolness, there is often a slight pressure, like that of a soft blanket lying against the skin. Sometimes it produces a prickling sensation that is like being pricked gently with the point of a needle. This sounds unpleasant, but it is not really painful. A spirit may also come as a soft weight on the body to those who are lying in bed.

This sense of weight on the chest sometimes occurs during a particular type of nightmare that was known as a visitation of the "night hag" because the spirit sometimes appears in the form of a horrible old woman, although more often the spirit remains invisible in the darkness. The person who experiences it finds it impossible to move, even after they become fully awake and aware.

Scientists dismiss this unpleasant experience with the term *sleep paralysis*, which is the natural inhibition of body movements during sleep that prevents sleeping persons from hurting themselves during dreams, but what does this term really explain about the visitation of the hag, which is so consistent and uniform in its various details? What does it explain about the distinct sensations of this spirit pressing down on your feet, climbing up your legs, or sitting on your chest and face to smother you? It explains nothing.

The exercises that follow concentrate mainly on developing your skills in sight scrying and, to a lesser degree, in sound scrying. When you develop ability in one form of scrying, you will find that your talent for other forms increases as well.

Your skill in visualization that you acquired from the exercises in the third chapter will prove to be a useful aid when learning how to scry. When we visualize, we imagine that we see or hear something in the mind. We all have a natural skill for doing this—it's called dreaming. After all, what is dreaming except scrying while asleep? Conversely, scrying may be described as dreaming while awake. Imagining sights and sounds can serve to prime the psychic pump, so to speak, and can help draw forth actual impressions of sights or sounds when we scry.

EXERCISES FOR CHAPTER 10

Exercise 10.1: Pattern Recognition

This is an exercise you can do when the opportunity presents itself. As you go about your daily activities, when you happen across a surface that has an irregular texture or pattern, stop and take a few minutes to stare at it with a relaxed, open mind. Some surfaces that work well are curtains, rugs, rumpled bed sheets, piles of clothes, patterned ceiling plaster, a roughly painted or concrete wall, freshly turned garden soil. Become aware of any recognizable faces or forms that seem to jump forth from the chaos of the general background pattern. Try to pick out as many shapes as you can.

Faces are usually the easiest thing to see in a textured or irregular surface because the human mind is hardwired to recognize faces. The faces will be distorted and may appear demonic due to this distortion. You will also find yourself making out buildings, animals, trees, flowers, birds, fish, dragons, and so on. You may even see complete scenes such as a house in a valley between two hills.

Some surfaces lend themselves better to pattern recognition than others. The texture or patterning of the surface needs to be irregular but evenly distributed, with a random scattering of ridges, curves, and shadows. Avoid regular patterns such as printed wallpaper, printed curtains, and wood grains—these usually do not yield good results, although sometimes varnished wooden doors can be rich in grotesque faces.

On a day when the clouds are fluffy and separated from each other by blue sky, take some time to sit or lie staring up at them with your mind relaxed. Try to think of nothing. Avoid any expectations about what you may see. Take mental note of any shapes you recognize. The things you see won't be perfectly formed, but the clouds will suggest their outline, or part of their outline. People sometimes refer to this as "seeing castles in the clouds." It's an activity that children delight in, and they have a natural aptitude for it. Do this for fifteen or twenty minutes at a time.

Exercise 10.2: Color Changes in a Crystal

In this exercise, you will be crystal gazing. You may see faces, figures, or scenes during your first attempt, but this is unlikely unless you have a strong, natural psychic talent. However, even beginners are able to observe changing colors in the crystal.

Set a crystal ball on a table and sit before it with the ball about four feet away from your head. The room should be dimly lit. A good time to do this exercise is at twilight. If you do it after sunset, light two candles and place them on the left and right sides of the crystal ball and about two feet away from it, so that the flames of the candles are not directly in the center of your field of vision. The light from the candles must not distract your attention away from the crystal ball.

If you don't own a crystal ball, you can do this exercise with a bowl of clear, plain water. A clear glass dessert bowl works well, but any small bowl made of clear, transparent glass will do. Fill the bowl on the table with water and sit down before it in a comfortable chair with your back straight, hands on your knees, and feet flat on the floor and about twelve inches apart.

Fix your gaze on the crystal ball or bowl of water without moving your attention away from it. Try not to blink too often. When your eyes begin to burn, close them and open them, but continue to stare at the crystal or bowl without shifting your gaze or losing focus. This exercise depends in part upon fatigue of the optic nerve, which is why you must not shift your gaze. After several minutes, or perhaps sooner, colors will come.

Each color covers the crystal, persists for a few seconds, then shifts to another color. The colors flow like oil from one to the next. They are vibrant colors, rich and deep, but uniform. You may see deep purple, forest green, blood red, sky blue, bright orange, pale mauve, and other colors. The colors that appear and their sequence of changes are not important for this exercise. Observe them come and go in the crystal or in the water with a passive, open mind.

Continue in this way for fifteen minutes or so, then close your eyes to relax them and take a few silent breaths to end the exercise.

Exercise 10.3: Scrying Auras

In the last chapter, you practiced visualizing your aura in various ways. This exercise is designed to awaken your psychic ability to actually scry the aura with your inner sight. Not everyone can see auras, but it is a useful skill to develop if you have the innate talent within you to do so. Once you understand how auras change and what their colors signify, you can use them to read the emotional states of others, the brooding tendency of their thoughts, even their state of physical health. Our auras proclaim to the world what we are hiding inside ourselves.

The easiest parts of the body to see auras around are the head and the hands. The aura shines forth most strongly from these parts, particularly from the face and head. This is why Christian saints are so often described as wearing a halo of light or as having a face that shines like the sun. The shining countenance, the halo, and the nimbus of saints are all manifestations of the aura, which we all possess but which shines forth more strongly from those who are spiritually enlightened.

In my own experience, I have found that the easiest condition under which to detect the aura is at twilight, when the air is a uniform gray and colors become dim. You can artificially create this light during the day by drawing the curtains to dim the room light. If the curtains are fairly heavy but do not block out all the light, this will produce the desired conditions. Or you can wait until it is actually twilight and do the exercise by the natural light coming in through the window. A very dark, overcast, rainy day will sometimes create the right lighting conditions.

Stand facing east, and draw a few silent breaths to relax and focus on what you are about to do.

It is easiest to detect the aura around your own hands. Hold your hands out in front of you about two feet away from your face and look at them against a gray or dim background. Look in particular at the edges of your separated fingers and at their tips.

The dim light will make the air seem to dance with tiny particles, as though little grains of gray sand were floating in the air. You should be able to make out a kind of wavering around the edges of your fingers. It looks something like ripples in the air created by heat rising from a paved road on a hot day. This shimmering and rippling of the air will extend about half an inch away from your fingers. It may be easier to see at your fingertips.

Play around with various slight changes in the intensity of the light and with different backgrounds if you don't see this effect immediately. When conditions are right, it is quite easy to see.

Continue in this way for five minutes or so, then resume the standing posture and take a few silent breaths to end the exercise.

Exercise 10.4: Wind Scrying

For this exercise in awakening your sound scrying ability, you will need a windy day and a location from which you can hear the wind blowing through the rustling leafy branches of a tree or trees. Adopt a sitting posture and listen for ten or fifteen minutes with your eyes closed.

You are listening for voices in the wind. Do not try to force your perceptions, but keep a passive, open mind with your attention on the sound of the rustling leaves. Take mental note of any individual words or short phrases you hear. The sound of the leaves provides the matrix upon which spirit voices can shape themselves.

It is important that there be no distracting noises to draw your attention away from the wind. You should not be thinking of anything else or feeling impatient, and you must not have what the magician Aleister Crowley called a "lust of result," or the voices in the wind will not make themselves known to you.[14] Do not anticipate any particular outcome—there is no success or failure in this exercise, only progress.

The spirits are always around you, and they are always trying to speak to you. By supplying them with a matrix upon which to shape their voices, you facilitate the communication they are seeking to establish. Wind scrying lends itself to communications from sylphs, the elemental spirits of the air. Sylphs are the most talkative of the four types of elementals, perhaps because words are shaped and carried on their native element.

Much depends on the conditions under which you wind scry. A strong, fitful breeze produces the greatest variety of sounds, but it must be constant enough to sustain voices for half a dozen seconds at a time so that the spirits have a chance to say something, even if it is only a word or two. The type of trees you sit under also matters—the louder and more varied the rustle, the better the effect.

I have specified trees, but wind scrying can be done anywhere the wind makes a sustained but variable sound—when it blows in a chimney, for example, or around the eve of a house on blustery days and nights.

Exercise 10.5: Pattern Making

In the first exercise of this chapter, you gained practice in recognizing meaningful shapes in random, chaotic backgrounds and

---

14. Aleister Crowley, *The Book of the Law* (South Stukely, Quebec: 93 Publishing, 1975), 20.

textures that you encounter around you. The present exercise involves creating your own patterns intuitively that will allow faces and forms to come forward into your consciousness.

You will need privacy and quiet. On a clear area of your kitchen countertop, sprinkle a light layer of flour, as though you were making bread and planned to knead the dough on the counter. It should not completely cover the counter but lie upon it in irregular overlapping patches, like fluffy white clouds in the sky.

Look down at the flour and relax your mind. Open yourself to visual impressions. Let your eyes wander over the irregular patches of flour and take note of any forms that may suggest themselves. Do this for at least several minutes.

With your fingertips, lightly brush the flour back and forth on the counter. Move your hand in curves and loops as well as short straight lines until there is a pattern of marks in the flour. Do not make these marks in any regular manner. Do not think about how you will move your hand before you start. Let your intuition inspire the movements of your fingertips over the flour.

Study the pattern you have created with a passive, open mind. You must not try to force yourself to see shapes in the flour—rather, you must allow these shapes time to present themselves to you. If you try to force them, they will not come. Take note of any faces, objects, structures, or beasts that suggest themselves to your mind.

Sprinkle fresh flour over the layer you have brushed with your fingertips, and do the same thing again, keeping your mind as empty and as receptive as possible. Study this second pattern of flour just as you did the first pattern. Be aware of any forms that seem to repeat themselves. Be conscious of whether the faces in the flour are angry, laughing, frightened, or grotesque. Observe whether the faces are human, animal, or otherworldly.

End this exercise by brushing the flour from your countertop and discarding it.

You can perform this same exercise out of doors using fine sand or soft soil instead of flour. The essential requirement is that you be able to create lines and ridges in the material with your fingertips that will suggest forms as you gaze on them.

Exercise 10.6: River Scrying

This is another sound scrying exercise. It requires that you be able to sit quietly and privately beside a stream, brook, or river, where it flows over rocks and creates a babbling sound. It is best to do this work alone, surrounded by the stillness of the forest and far enough away from other human beings that you cannot hear them or their machines.

In my experience, the babble of flowing water over stones is the best sound matrix for scrying spirit voices. I find it difficult to avoid hearing voices talking to me when I walk beside a stream.

River scrying lends itself to communications from undines, the class of spirit associated with elemental water. These spirits are very sociable and enjoy interacting with human beings. They dwell around freshwater springs, streams, pools, and rivers and in particular favor quiet, shaded glades.

Sit or lie beside the water. Close your eyes to help free your mind from visual distractions. Listen to the babbling water as it tumbles over stones until you begin to distinguish voices speaking amid the sounds. At first, you will receive only fragments of words or phrases, but some words may be startlingly clear to you.

When the water begins to speak to you in this way, chant the following incantation:

Spirits of water, talk to me;
Teach me all I seek to know.
Reveal the secrets kept by thee;
The Goddess wills it, make it so.

Lie in silence for a short while, then ask the spirits of the stream a question and wait for their response. It will come in the form of a word or several words that you hear clearly amid the babbling of the water over the stones.

Continue in this way, asking questions that arise in your mind and waiting for the response of the spirits. Take mental note of what they say to you, even if their words do not appear to make meaningful sense at the time you hear them.

To end the exercise, thank the spirits, open your eyes, and leave the waterside.

It is useful to write down your questions and the responses given by the undines while both are fresh in your mind, because at a later date words that appeared meaningless at the time you received them may take on important significance in relation to the changing events in your life.

Exercise 10.7: Moon Scrying

The moon has always been closely linked with scrying. The qualities needed for scrying are for the most part lunar qualities—receptiveness, imagination, tranquility, visualization. To scry, the mind must become like the mirror surface of a lake, undisturbed by ripples of thought or desire.

This method of scrying is ancient. It was used by the Greeks in their mystery schools and has been adopted in modern times by witches who worship the lunar goddess. It should be done when the moon is full, or nearly full, and visible high in the night sky.

You will need a small basin or bowl. Ideally, it should be made of solid silver or silver plated. Alternatively, you can use a bowl of transparent, colorless glass. Both silver and glass are strongly lunar substances. You will also need a leaf-bearing wand that has been freshly cut from a living tree. A good choice of tree for this purpose is the willow, due to its love for water, but apple, cherry, birch, maple, laurel, and most other leaf-bearing trees will serve. Choose a young shoot or sapling with small leaves. Shortly before you do this exercise, cut the wand from the tree so that the leaves are fresh.

Set the bowl and the wand on a table that is placed under a window through which the moon shines or outside in the open air where the moonlight can fall upon it. Fill the bowl with clean water.

Sit in a plain kitchen chair at the table in such a way that the moon in the night sky above you is reflected in the surface of the water in the bowl, so that you can see the moon in the water.

Relax and close your eyes. Take several silent breaths to calm your mind, then open your eyes.

Pick up the wand by its freshly cut end and dip its leafy tip in the water of the bowl, then flick it to your left side so that droplets of water fly off it to the left. Do the same thing and flick it to your right side. Dip the wand a third time and flick the water forward in front of you. Dip it again, and flick the water back over your left shoulder. Speak this ritual formula:

Move not, for the place is holy.

Use the tip of the wand to slowly stir the surface of the water in the bowl in a clockwise direction. As you do so, visualize a clockwise spiral on the surface of the water and recite this incantation:

Diana, Selene, Hecate,
Descend, descend, descend to me;
Into this bowl your shining face,
Fill with light this sacred space.

Set the wand down on the table and gaze at the reflected image of the moon in the surface of the water in the bowl as it ceases to ripple and becomes still. Open your mind to its silver light. Be aware that the goddess of the moon, who is a threefold goddess of many names, is now present in the water. Keep your gaze fixed on the reflection, but with your mind, look through and beyond the image of the moon to what lies behind it. Project your awareness through the moon.

As the moon moves in the sky, you will need to adjust your position slightly from time to time to keep the image of the moon centered in the bowl. Continue to scry with a passive, receptive mind, and take note of any impressions that suggest themselves, any thoughts that arise, or memories that suddenly come forward. Do this for twenty minutes or so.

If nothing seems to come into your mind that is meaningful, and you see no visions in the water, do not be discouraged. The process itself is awakening your latent natural scrying abilities and strengthening them. Oftentimes what arises in the mind seems unimportant at the time, but its significance reveals itself days later.

To end the exercise, take up the wand and tap the surface of the water lightly three times. Each time you tap the water, say one of the names of the lunar goddess as you recite the following words:

Diana, Selene, Hecate,
Depart in peace and go your way.

Lay down the wand across the top of the bowl. Close your eyes and draw several silent breaths, then open your eyes and rise from your seat to end the exercise.

Exercise 10.8: Clay Shaping

You will need some soft modeling clay that is easily worked with your hands. There should be enough to form a ball about the size of an orange. A few simple modeling tools may be used to help shape the clay, such as a pencil and a butter knife, but these are not essential—you can do the exercise with only your fingers.

Place the clay on a table on some open newspapers or other papers that will protect the table, and sit down. Take several silent breaths to focus your thoughts.

Begin to squeeze and work the clay between your hands. Focus your gaze on it, but keep your mind empty and receptive. Twist, elongate, flatten, and shape the clay with no desire for a result in mind. Allow the clay to show you what it wants to be. When you get a sense that the clay should be shaped a certain way, shape it that way.

The clay may turn itself into a figure, a bird, a beast, or a geometric shape. Allow the clay to express itself, and try not to get in the way of that expression. Feel the sensuality of it moving between your fingers as you shape it. Almost it seems to possess a life of its own.

You will often find as you shape the clay that a face begins to develop. If this occurs, allow the face to emerge from the clay as you mold it.

When the clay attains a form that you intuitively sense is right for it, place it on the table, sit upright in your chair, and contemplate the clay with your hands on your knees. If you feel that something needs to be changed, make the changes in its shape and continue your contemplation. Do this for ten minutes or so.

Clay is the natural environment of the earth elementals known as gnomes. They are dwarflike beings with expressive but grotesque faces. Do not be surprised if such an elemental spirit communicates its presence to you through the clay. You should give permission to the spirit of the clay to speak to you. It will do so on a level below the level of words with its form, its pattern of light and shade, its curves and angles.

To conclude the exercise, thank the spirit of the clay, press the clay back into a ball, and set it aside. Take several silent breaths, then rise and go about your day.

Exercise 10.9: Fire Gazing

This is a very ancient form of scrying and a tradition in northern countries. I was taught fire scrying as a young child by my mother, who learned it from my grandfather. You will need a source of open flames such as a fireplace, a barbecue pit, or a campfire for this exercise.

Build a wood fire and allow the flames to blaze up and partially consume the wood so that a good bed of glowing embers is created beneath the burning logs. The best results will be obtained with a combination of glowing embers and flickering flames.

Sit before the fire in a comfortable position and fix your gaze on the embers. Take a few silent breaths to relax your mind, then open yourself to impressions from the fire. Be aware of the dance of the flames, of the changes in color from deep red to glowing white as air currents pass over the embers, of the sound of the flames fluttering and the wood crackling and sparking.

If images begin to suggest themselves in the fire, do not focus your mind on them, but remain passive and receptive. When you turn your mind to them, they will vanish. See them, be passively aware of them, but do not try to look directly at them. Allow impressions to gather in your mind.

These impressions will consist not only of images but of emotions, thoughts, and memories that arise as you look into the flames. All are important, all a part of the scrying.

Fire is the element of the salamanders, elemental beings whose bodies are composed of fire. You may see one dancing among the flames. Their movements are very abrupt and quick. They seldom use words to communicate with human beings and are the most difficult of the elementals with whom to interact.

Continue gazing into the fire for fifteen or twenty minutes. When it begins to burn itself down, close your eyes and take a few silent breaths to cleanse your mind, then open your eyes to end the exercise.

Exercise 10.10: Mirror Scrying

Sit in front of a mirror at least large enough to reflect an image of your entire face. The room should be dark, with a single candle burning directly behind you, so that your face is shadowed in the mirror and the edges of your head and body are illuminated by the light behind your back. You must create a lighting condition where you can see your own features in the mirror, but only in a dim way. Take a few deep, silent breaths to prepare.

Scry into the image of your face in the mirror. Keep your mind open and receptive. Look upon the reflection as something completely separate and apart from you. Without actually thinking about it, hold in your mind the understanding that the room reflected in the mirror is not the room you occupy, the form in the mirror is not your body, and the face dimly visible in the mirror is not your face. They are the face, body, and room in some other dimension of reality.

Keep your gaze fixed on the right eye of the mirror image, and refrain from blinking as much as you can without straining your eyes. After a few minutes, fatigue of your optic nerve will cause the background reflected in the mirror to darken. You will see moving shapes in the shadows. Do not be alarmed by them—they are in the mirror, which is separate and distinct from the room in which you sit.

The expression of the face in the mirror will change and become distorted. It will begin to move. You may see the corners of the lips quirk into a smile, the eyes blink or widen, the head nod, the lips part.

When the face begins to change and move, you can ask questions of the figure in the mirror. Ask your questions in your mind, without speaking aloud. Responses will come in the form of slight movements of the face and head. The expression of the shadowed face may become happy or sad, fearful or angry, as you question it. You must interpret each change in expression in relation to the question you have just asked.

To end the exercise, nod to the image in the mirror to express your thanks. Stand up and turn on the room light. Blow out the candle. Avoid looking at the mirror. You may wish to drape a towel or other cloth over it to cover it. Turn your mind to everyday thoughts, and if it is convenient, go out of the room for a while.

CHAPTER 11
CHANNELING

Channeling differs from scrying in that it involves complete or partial control by a spirit over your body. Scrying can be done with no spirit possession of any kind. The two activities are closely related, but this distinction must be made between them—*scrying is perception of information; channeling is communication of information.* The scryer perceives; the channeler receives.

Channeling can be useful in magic because it allows spirits to express themselves in an articulate way that can be easily understood. If you are a magician who is not skilled at scrying and cannot easily see spirits or hear them speak to you, you can encourage them to communicate with you through various forms of channeling.

When we hear the word *channeling*, what we usually think of is a discarnate spirit taking full possession of a human being and speaking to others using the voice of the person possessed. We've all seen videos of channelers, and some of us have watched them in real life. The spirits possessing their bodies usually do not move around, but merely speak, and the channeler usually has no recollection of what the spirits said during the possession.

The most famous example of this modern form of channeling is that of the alien intelligence Seth, who took control over the channeler Jane Roberts to deliver a series of messages to the world. Roberts began communicating with Seth in 1963 by using a Ouija board. Eventually, she was able to channel Seth directly. Her first book completely dictated by this being, *Seth Speaks*, was published in 1972. In the first chapter of this book, Seth described himself as an "energy personality essence, no longer focused in physical matter."[15]

CHANNELING AND MEDIUMSHIP

This type of channeling is called *mediumship* by Spiritualists. Spiritualism is a religious movement that began in the first half of the nineteenth century and reached its height in the early decades of the twentieth century. It still exists today in a diminished form. There are Spiritualist churches where believers congregate to receive messages from their beloved dead.

The core of Spiritualist belief is that the dead do not completely vanish from our world but continue to observe and interact with the living. They remain invisible to most people, but some individuals who are psychically gifted are able to see and hear them, and these psychics offer their bodies as vehicles through which the dead can speak, by using their voices. When they do so, they become "mediums" for the spirits of the dead, conduits through which the spirits convey messages to the living.

Modern channeling is just mediumship stripped of the religious and ritual trappings of Spiritualism. The same thing is happening for both channelers and spirit mediums—bodiless beings

15. Jane Roberts, *Seth Speaks: The Eternal Validity of the Soul* (Englewood Cliffs, NJ: Prentice-Hall, 1972), 5.

take partial or full possession of these psychics in order to speak through them to other human beings.

Some channelers will claim that the entities they channel are living corporeal beings who are far removed in distance—enlightened masters in Tibet, for example, or aliens living on other planets, or even beings in other dimensions of reality. There is no objective way to demonstrate the truth of such assertions, which are made by the spirits themselves.

One of the first things you learn in magic is that spirits do not always tell the truth. Sometimes they make statements that are in error, sometimes they tell lies, and sometimes they actually speak the truth in complete and accurate detail. It requires discernment on the part of the magician to determine when a spirit is being truthful and when its words cannot be trusted. Information from spirits on practical matters should always be checked and verified against known facts, whenever this is possible. You should never take any radical action in your life based solely on the words of a spirit.

Full possession is not something that is encouraged in modern magic. The point of becoming a magician, in the traditional archetypal sense, is to gain control over esoteric forces and spiritual beings, to master and command them by being in command of yourself. Of course, there are many today who study magic with less aggressive intentions, but magic at its root is about mastery—mastering skills, spells, forces, spirits, even gods. This is out of keeping with full possession, during which the spirit displaces the consciousness of the medium, or channeler, and takes complete control over his or her body.

METHODS OF PARTIAL POSSESSION

For this reason, the methods of channeling I will teach in this chapter do not involve full possession. You will not lose consciousness when you practice these exercises, nor will you lose control over your own body. The spirits who communicate with you will take partial and temporary control over a portion of your body in order to use it to communicate with you by the motions of objects or through images and written words.

You should engage in channeling only with spirits who are polite, well-behaved, and intelligent. If a spirit initiating communication with you is vulgar, threatening, or abusive in any way, or if you sense deception on the spirit's part, you should break communication with that spirit and state clearly that you wish the spirit to depart and not return.

The methods of partial channeling examined here involve the casting of lots, the dowsing rod, the pendulum, the Ouija board, automatic drawing, and automatic writing. In all cases, the communicating spirit takes temporary control over a portion of your body and uses it to communicate while you retain full awareness of what is happening around you.

Channeling is a useful skill in magic, particularly when you are not enough advanced in your practice to hear the words of spirits spoken to you directly. In order to interact with spiritual beings in the most efficient manner as a magician, it is necessary not only that you be able to communicate with them, but that they can communicate back to you. Conveying your words to spirits is easy because spirits perceive your thoughts when you shape them clearly in your own mind. They also hear you when you speak to them aloud. But perceiving the words that spirits speak to you is far more difficult and uncommon. These forms of partial channeling will allow spirits to express themselves to you and to convey useful teachings. It is well worth the effort to acquire these skills.

Casting Lots

The fall of lots is an oracle in which you cast objects on the ground or on a table and observe how they lie. Cleromancy (Latin: *cleromantia*) means to divine by lots. Throwing a set of dice is a form of lot casting. In ancient times, dice were used as an oracle, but they became debased into an instrument for gambling. Many different objects may be used for lots, such as beans, stones, twigs, and bones that are shaped, marked, or colored in ways that distinguish one from another or one side from another. Lots may also be drawn, by blindly selecting one or more from a larger group.

The casting or drawing of lots is mentioned in both the Old and New Testaments. The Urim and Thummim were used in this way by the High Priest of the Hebrews. The Roman soldiers present at the crucifixion cast lots (presumably dice) to decide which of them would get the clothing of Jesus after his death. The apostles drew lots to determine who would replace Judas, after Judas killed himself.

It was the custom of the ancient Greeks to mark Greek letters onto tokens and place them in an urn. Some of the tokens were then thrown out of the urn and scattered on the ground, and the way in which they fell was interpreted. Meaning was probably derived not only from the letters, which were read in different orderings to form words, but also from the pattern of the tokens.

It may seem at first consideration that the casting of lots has nothing to do with channeling, but both channeling and lot casting involve information received from a spirit through the manipulation of a human being. The theory behind casting lots is that a god or other higher intelligence will influence the fall of the lots in order to convey an answer to a question.

In the past, the assumption was often made that the spirit influenced the lot itself to fall a certain way, but the lot is an inanimate object. Spirits have a hard time affecting inanimate objects but a relatively easy time manipulating human beings. What actually happens is that the spirit influences the body of the person casting the lots to achieve the result the spirit intends.

Almost anything can be used for lots once you establish a few simple rules for how they are to be interpreted after they are cast. If the lots are two-sided, one side can signify a positive response and the other side a negative response. This oracle works best when you are seeking yes or no to a specific question, but the rules of interpretation can be adapted to yield more complex information. For example, a lot falling close to the person who casts it can indicate nearness in space or time of the matter under question; a lot that falls farther away can indicate a greater distance in time or space; two lots falling together can be interpreted as two aspects of the matter that are conjoined or linked in some way; a lot that falls on top of another lot can be said to dominate it; and so on.

Ouija Board

Some of you reading this may have heard bad things about the Ouija board. The evils of the board have been greatly exaggerated. It is a very useful tool for receiving communications from spiritual beings, and it has the virtue of working, at least to some degree, for almost everyone who tries it with an honest and open mind. This is the reason the board has acquired such an evil reputation—because it actually does work, and when people see evidence of the spirit world for the first time with their own eyes, they are often terrified.

The talking board, as it is sometimes called, is quite ancient. It was not invented by Elijah J. Bond in 1890. It was used by the Greeks and Romans in a different form before the time of Christ, and during the nineteenth century, it was a popular Victorian parlor game. The practice of the Victorians was to mark the letters of the alphabet on small cards and place the cards in a circle on a smooth table. A glass was inverted and used as a pointer to select individual letters to make up the words of a message. Those playing this game stood or sat around the table, and each person rested a finger on the end of the glass, which soon began to move in response to questions.

Elijah Bond's innovation was to paint the alphabet on a rectangular board in two crescent rows, along with numerals from zero to nine beneath the letters, the words *yes* and *no* in the upper corners, and the words *good bye* at the bottom center of the board. He also designed a wooden pointer roughly in the shape of a frying pan with a pointed handle and four long legs. The point of the handle indicated the letters on the board, as is clearly shown in Bond's February 10, 1891, patent illustration. This proved to be a workable arrangement, and the "Ouija or Egyptian luck-board," as Bond called his innovation in his patent, has remained popular ever since.[16]

I've done a fair amount of occult work with various versions of the talking board. Over the years, I've made three of them that are roughly based on Bond's design, and I've used both an older and a newer commercial model from Parker Brothers. My general conclusion is that the old method of using a circle of numbers and an upturned glass on a smooth surface, such as a dining table, is

---

16. Patent number 446,054. The patent application with illustrations may be downloaded as a PDF from Google Patents: https://patents.google.com/patent/US446054A/en.

superior. The most important factor is that the pointer slides freely, so the surface must be perfectly smooth.

Dowsing

The dowsing rod and the pendulum are very closely related. Indeed, the pendulum was often used in place of a rod to dowse for water, lost objects, and things buried under the ground. The supposition was that a spirit moved the pendulum. Dowsing is many centuries old. It was used by miners in Europe in the sixteenth and seventeenth centuries to find veins of metal. Indeed, it was the standard practice of miners to employ dowsers for this purpose. In later centuries, it became usual for a dowser to be employed to locate the best spot to dig a water well. Dowsing is still used for this today.

Modern dowsers usually do not understand that a spirit is guiding the movements of their rod. They considered dowsing an inherent talent, similar to the second sight of the Celts. Those who employ the pendulum as a dowsing instrument hold a similar belief, but the pendulum is also sometimes used to gain communications from spirits by noting its motions and deriving a yes or a no to questions depending on how the pendulum swings.

The ancient Greeks used a pendulum to point out the letters of the Greek alphabet that were inscribed around the rim of a large basin or bowl.This method, which is somewhat similar to the way the Ouija board works, yielded enigmatic oracles in the form of verse that had to be interpreted for their meaning, just as the verse oracles delivered verbally by the prophetess at Delphi, who was known as the Pythia, had to be interpreted by priests skilled in this art.

Automatic Writing and Drawing

Automatic writing is the practice of sitting down with a pencil and a sheet of paper and opening your mind to allow a spirit to use your arm and hand to make marks on the paper. These may be written words, or in the beginning they may only be lines and squiggles. It requires some practice on the part of a spirit before it can control a channeler's hand well enough to produce actual automatic script that can be read and understood. However, with practice, spirits are able to write fluently.

It is possible to converse with the medium while this is going on, since the medium's conscious mind is not engaged in the writing. Spirits have written entire published books in this way, by using human mediums as their instruments. This form of spirit literature was particularly popular in the second half of the nineteenth century when Spiritualism was in vogue. I have been able to collect a small library of such works consisting of spirit poetry, spirit novels, spirit essays, prophecies, and spiritual teachings of various kinds.

Automatic drawing is the transmission of symbolic shapes or images. It is similar to automatic writing, but a different part of the mind is engaged, the part that deals with pictures instead of spoken words. At first, attempts at automatic drawing are crude, but they should not be dismissed since even at this stage they often contain symbolic elements of value and convey important information. With practice, a skilled channeler is able to produce complex drawings and paintings without effort and with no conscious participation.

IS CHANNELING DANGEROUS?

A little reflection will show that the casting of lots, the use of the dowsing rod, the pendulum, and the talking board all require that the hand and arm of the person working them be taken over by an intelligence other than the conscious intelligence of the person. The users of these devices do not deliberately move them to gain responses from them—the devices seem to move on their own.

We might debate the identity of this other intelligence that moves the device. Is it the higher self of the user? Is it a dead relative or the ghost of a stranger? An angel? An alien being from another dimension? An enlightened mystic somewhere else in the world? A dormant second personality within the mind of the user? A demon that has taken up residence in the device? God? Satan?

The general belief of those who use the Ouija is that spirits move the pointer on the talking board—sometimes the spirits of the dead, and sometimes spirit beings who were never living. Devout Christians claim that the devil moves the pointer. If so, he is doing very little with this ability, because the Ouija board, along with lot casting, the pendulum, and the dowsing rod, has proved over the course of many centuries to be harmless to those who are stable mentally.

Nervous people unfamiliar with interacting with spirits will sometimes frighten themselves quite badly with the Ouija board and imagine all kinds of dire consequences from using it. If there were any real danger, it would not have remained a parlor amusement for adults and a game for children over so many generations. Those not accustomed to receiving spirit communications are often terrified to discover that all this "occult stuff," which they always dismissed as nonsense, is actually real.

If you are nervous about using the Ouija or other forms of the talking board, I advise you to practice channeling only with lots, the dowsing rod, and the pendulum and also to experiment with the techniques of automatic drawing and writing.

EXERCISES FOR CHAPTER 11

Exercise 11.1: Casting of Lots

You will need three coins for lots. Any sort of coin will do, but all three should be the same. A fall of a coin with heads up will be interpreted as a yes and with tails up as a no. To prepare the coins, wash them in clean water and anoint them with virgin olive oil, then dry them on a clean white cloth.

On a slip of paper, write the question to which you seek an answer. Be explicit in your wording of the question so that a yes or a no will provide you with a useful response.

Place the coins and the question on a table. Also on the table have a candle in a holder and a fireproof saucer or other small plate. Light the candle. The room should be darkened so that the flame of the candle provides the main source of illumination.

Sit at the table facing the east, if possible, with the coins in front of you. If you cannot face east, do not worry about the direction you face; it is a minor matter. Close your eyes and take several silent breaths to calm and focus your mind.

Press your palms together and raise them in front of your forehead in a gesture of prayer. Speak an invocation to whichever god, goddess, or angel you wish to respond to your question.

In this exercise, we will invoke the presence of the Greek god Hermes, who in ancient times was famed for his oracles. You do not need to use the exact words of the following invocation, but you should express your sincere desire that the spirit invoked attend on your casting of the lots and guide them to give you a true answer to your question.

Wise Hermes, messenger of the gods, grant me a true answer to my question. Guide my hands so that these coins fall as you intend,

and banish my uncertainty so that I may interpret their fall rightly.
In return, I offer the value of these coins to you for your service.

Open your eyes, take up the slip of paper with your question written on it, and read it aloud. Then light the paper and let it burn until it is completely consumed by fire. Drop the last corner of burning paper onto the saucer so that you do not burn your fingers. Make sure that all the writing of your question has burned. If a blank corner of paper is left over, it does not matter.

Take up the coins and shake them between your cupped palms. Extend your hands outward over the tabletop at a height of six or eight inches above the table, then open your hands downward as though opening the covers of a book, so that the coins fall straight down onto the table.

Do not drop them from a greater height, or the coins may roll off the table—you want them to fall cleanly from your hands but not to roll onto the floor. If you place a white towel on the table, this will tend to inhibit the coins from rolling away. If by chance one or more of the coins does roll off the table, the oracle of the lots is spoiled, and you must abort it and try again at another time.

The way to interpret the coins is this—three heads means an emphatic yes to your question, but three tails means an emphatic no; two heads means yes, but less completely; and two tails mean no, but not so emphatic a negative as three tails. If a coin with heads is the nearest coin to you on the table, it signifies that the outcome of the question, whether positive or negative, will occur in the near future; if the nearest coin shows tails, it indicates that the outcome is more distant. Also, if the coins are close together, the outcome will be definite and cohesive, but if they are scattered apart, the outcome will be ragged and irregular.

After interpreting the fall of the coins, once again make the gesture of prayer and give thanks to Hermes, in these or similar words:

Noble Hermes, I thank you for your presence and for your guidance in the matter here decided. Depart, and peace be with you.

Take a few silent breaths to end the exercise. Open your eyes, gather up the coins, and bury them in the earth in some convenient place where they will not be disturbed. Put them completely out of your mind, and never dig them up. They are your payment to Hermes for his answer to your question.

Exercise 11.2: Ouija Board

For this exercise, you will need a Ouija board and the help of another person. It is a curious aspect of the Ouija that two or more people can cause it to work quickly and easily, in most cases, but a single person alone often has no success.

Sit facing the other person on plain kitchen chairs. Place the board so that it is supported by your knees and the knees of the person who is helping you. It doesn't matter how the board is oriented, but you may wish to turn it so that the letters and numbers are upright from your perspective.

The best way to start is with questions that can be answered by a simple yes or no. After the pointer begins to move freely, you can ask more complex questions that require a word or a phrase in response. Because the pointer spells out words letter by letter, you do not want to ask questions that require a lengthy response. It is easy to mistake which letter the pointer is indicating, and you can lose your place in a long response, which then becomes a meaningless string of letters.

Rest the pointer in the center of the board and place the index and middle fingers of your hand on it. Have your friend do the same. You may use either hand—experiment to find which hand works best for you. Do not press hard. Move the pointer in clockwise circles to get the feel of its motion, then change to counterclockwise circles. Now cause the pointer to describe figure eights on the board.

When you have loosened up your arm in this way for a minute or two, you may ask your first question:

Are any spirits present?

Continue to move the pointer lightly in figure eights, pausing its motion from time to time for a short while to see if it is reacting. You should repeat the question, allowing time for any spirit who may seek to influence the board to respond. Continue in this way until you feel the pointer begin to move by itself.

This feeling is distinct and unmistakable. The pointer will appear to move slowly and haltingly under its own power, completely independent of your touch upon it. Maintain a light but constant contact with the pointer as it moves, and allow it to find its own direction.

It is usually not difficult to tell when the other person is trying to deceive you by forcing the motion of the pointer. It will move more strongly and more deliberately than is common at the beginning of the communication. Most beginners automatically assume that the other person is cheating and pushing the pointer deliberately, because they cannot believe that it is actually moving on its own, as it appears to do. The impression produced by the movement of the pointer is uncanny—it feels exactly as though the pointer itself is moving.

Oftentimes, when beginners use the Ouija, the first movements of the pointer are awkward and random, as the spirit struggles to gain control over its direction by manipulating your muscles and the muscles of the person helping you. As the session progresses, the motions of the pointer become stronger and more certain.

Ask if there are any spirits present. When there is a response, ask whether it was once a living human being. Ask if it is a man or a woman. When the movements of the pointer become more confident, ask it to spell out its name.

As you ask your questions, a second spirit may take over the movement of the pointer from the spirit that initially appeared. You will be able to tell this transition by the different nature of the pointer's movements.

Continue asking questions until you wish to stop or until the responses of the spirit become erratic. Tell the spirit that you are ending the communication and wish it well, then say goodbye to it. Wait to see if the spirit will move the pointer to the words *good bye* at the bottom of the board.

Usually, it will do so. If it does not, don't be alarmed. Bear in mind that the spirit moving the pointer was present before it spoke to you through the board, so its continuing presence is not anything to be greatly concerned about. But most often spirits will have the courtesy to say goodbye to you.

Exercise 11.3: Ring of Letters

You don't need to buy a commercial Ouija board in order to practice this kind of channeling. You can easily make your own board out of a few scraps of paper and a small glass.

The most important factor when making this Victorian-style talking board is a smooth table. The glass must be able to slide across the table with almost no effort. The table must be small enough that people can sit around it and reach across it but large enough to accommodate the ring of letters.

Cut twenty-eight pieces of cardboard or paper, each around two inches wide and three inches long. When cut into three pieces, the standard index card yields rectangles of thin cardboard that work well, but you can use any paper you wish.

With a felt-tipped marker, make a capital letter of the alphabet on twenty-six of the rectangles. Write the words *yes* and *no* on the other two pieces of cardboard.

Order the letters of the alphabet in a circle that is around eighteen inches in diameter. It needs to be small enough that everyone participating can easily reach across to its far side while sitting around the table. Position the *yes* and *no* in between letters on opposite sides of the circle so that they form part of the circle. Tape down the letters with Scotch tape to prevent them from moving if you brush against them.

For the pointer, you will need a small glass, the smaller the better. A whisky shot glass works the best, in my experience, but any small glass will do, such as a small wine glass. Place it upside down in the center of the circle. Your homemade talking board is now ready to use.

Sit at the table and take a few slow, silent breaths to focus and relax. Place two fingers on the end of the glass. If there are several people participating, there may only be room on the glass for a single finger each. Don't worry about it. Because the glass is round and does not need to be oriented to point at the letters, one finger is enough.

The ring of letters is used the same way as the Ouija board. Take a few slow, silent breaths to calm yourself, then place your fingers on the glass and move it in circles for a minute or two.

You can reverse the direction of the circles from time to time or describe figure eights with the glass.

Do not try to force the glass. Let the glass move by itself. Keep your touch upon it light but constant. Empty your mind of desire or expectation and open your awareness. Ask your first question clearly, and word it in such a way that it can be answered by a yes or a no. Allow ample time for any spirit who may be present to answer. It may take the spirit several minutes to learn how to move the glass, or even longer.

Ask your questions clearly, and do not overlay them. Never ask one question right after another. Even if you are practicing alone, it is best to speak your questions out loud so that they are very clear in your own mind. Spirits can read your thoughts when you voice them in your mind, but if you speak them out loud, they will be even clearer to the spirits.

When you are finished, thank any spirits who may be present and say goodbye to them. Do this even if you have not received a response. It is always best to be serious and polite when dealing with spiritual beings, and you should always assume that spirits are present around you.

This kind of channeling works very easily for two or several people, but it is much more difficult for a single person to master. You should do this exercise at the same time each day for several weeks before you become discouraged. If you find that you cannot get results on your own, enlist the help of another person you can trust to take the exercise seriously and not cheat by deliberately pushing the glass. Results are usually very easy for two people working together.

Exercise 11.4: Pendulum

The pendulum is an ancient form of channeling. It was used by the Greeks and Romans as a form of divination and is popular in modern magic for the same purpose. It is a dual-purpose oracle—it can be used to locate lost or hidden items and to find water or minerals under the ground, but it can also be used to converse with spirits.

You can make a pendulum yourself out of a small object and a length of thread. The best materials for the object are lunar materials because you will use it to receive impressions and communications on a subconscious level, and this is a lunar function. Glass, crystal, and silver work well. You can also use lunar stones such as moonstone, jet, obsidian, or pearl.

Something such as a silver ring or a silver earring works quite well. If the object is too light, it will get blown around by any breeze and will not pull the thread taut, which will cause it to move erratically, making it unreliable. Conversely, if the object is too heavy, the spirits will not be able to set it into motion easily and it will seem to be unresponsive. I once tried to use a carpenter's plumb bob suspended on a chain for a pendulum but found that it was far too heavy for this purpose.

The object should be tied to a short length of white or black button thread. Thread works better than string, which is too thick to give good responses. Around eighteen inches of thread is sufficient.

For this exercise in using the pendulum to locate an object, you will need a deck of cards. Take out the four kings and the ace of spades from the deck. Shuffle these five cards together with your eyes closed and spread them out on a table face down so that they form a line with around six inches of space between adjacent cards.

Stand before the table with the pendulum in your hand. You can use either hand—try them both and find which hand works best for you. Wrap the end of the thread around your index finger so that the bob of the pendulum hangs down around eighteen inches. Wrapping the end of the thread around your finger makes it easier to hold for long periods of time and also causes a good contact to be made between your hand and the thread.

Take a few silent breaths with your eyes shut to focus and calm your mind. Open your eyes and speak your intention aloud firmly and clearly.

Spirit of the pendulum, find the ace.

Begin at one end of the row of cards by holding the pendulum a few inches above the card. Watch how the pendulum behaves. After a minute or so, move the pendulum to the next card in the row and repeat the observation. Do this for all five cards. If your mind is passive and open, the pendulum will move more energetically when it is above the ace.

Practice this exercise at the same time of day in the same place for several weeks in order to achieve the best results, and do not be discouraged if you interpret the pendulum incorrectly. Skill comes with practice.

Exercise 11.5: Pendulum and Glass

You will need a large empty water glass. Place it on a table and sit before it with the pendulum in your hand. Adjust the length of the thread and your hand position so that when you rest your elbow on the table, the bob of the pendulum dangles inside the glass and about halfway down its length. Hold it so that the bob is very close to the side of the glass but does not quite touch it.

As usual, you should take a few silent breaths to focus your mind before beginning. You can ask questions of spirits in the same way you did using the Ouija and the ring of letters, but all the questions must be answerable with either a yes or a no. If the answer is yes, the bob of the pendulum will *tink* against the inside of the glass; if the response is no, it will not produce a sound.

If you know the name of the spirit you wish to work with, use that name to address the spirit, but if you are just seeking a general response, address your questions to the spirit of the pendulum.

A familiar spirit will take up residence in the pendulum as you continue to use it. You will find that the more you practice, the more accurate the result. Next to the Ouija board, the pendulum is the easiest method of channeling from which to get a response.

It's best to practice this exercise in the same place and at the same time of day. You should persist for at least several weeks before you get discouraged. Almost everyone can get results from the pendulum. Experiment holding the pendulum with either hand, and try different hand and arm positions, different glasses, different lengths of the thread, and different separations between the pendulum and the inside of the glass until you find what works best for you.

Exercise 11.6: Pendulum and Circle

On a sheet of paper, draw a circle that is around six inches in diameter. Make a vertical line through the circle from top to bottom and a horizontal line from left to right so that the two lines cross in the center of the circle.

Sit at a table with the circle in front of you and rest your elbow on the table so that you can hold your pendulum directly above the center of the circle on its length of thread. The bob of the pendulum should be suspended around an inch above the circle. The left side of the body is receptive, so I recommend that you start by holding the pendulum in your left hand. However, you should experiment with both hands to find the side that works best for you.

Take a few silent breaths to focus your mind on what you are about to do. Allow the pendulum to swing unhindered above the cross for a minute or two.

All your questions must be worded so that they can be answered by either a yes or a no. This form of channeling will give a response of yes, no, or maybe. When the pendulum starts to swing up and down along the vertical line, the response is yes. When it swings from side to side above the horizontal line, the answer is no. If the pendulum swings in little circles around the center of the cross, this should be interpreted as maybe or uncertain. Decide clearly in your mind what each movement of the pendulum means before you begin.

Ask your questions of the spirit of the pendulum. A spirit who is present with you at the time of the exercise will take partial control over your arm and hand and cause the pendulum to move in a way that will give you meaningful answers to your questions.

You must allow the spirit sufficient time to take control of the pendulum. Ask only one question at a time and wait for several minutes for the spirit's response. Then ask another question and wait for the response. If you rush your questions, the responses will become meaningless.

Before beginning this exercise, decide on several questions that you would like answered. It may be useful to write them down. You can also ask spontaneous follow-up questions during the exercise as they occur to you.

It is important that you clearly understand and hold in your mind which motions of the pendulum will signify a yes and which motion will signify a no answer. I think of the up-and-down swinging of the pendulum as akin to a nodding of the head in affirmation and the side-to-side motion as a shaking of the head in negation. This is an easy way to remember which motion of the pendulum means yes and which means no.

When you have asked a dozen questions or so, thank the spirit of the pendulum for its participation even if the session has not been very enlightening. Set the pendulum down and take a few silent breaths to end.

Exercise 11.7: Dowsing Pencil

A simple dowsing rod can be achieved by using a plain wooden pencil. It should be sharp on the end and quite long—do not use a pencil that has been frequently sharpened. It is best to use a pencil that is hexagonal rather than one that is round.

You can use either hand, but I recommend that you start with your left hand. Curl the fingers of your hand slightly and balance the pencil across the side of your index finger in the crease between the first and second segments of your finger. The sharp end of the pencil should point forward, away from you. Keep your thumb out of the way.

It may take you a few seconds to find the exact balance point so that the pencil does not fall off, but once you do, it will be fairly stable, and you should be able to gently move your hand around without losing the pencil.

As an exercise, dowse for some object in your house that you have misplaced, such as your car keys or wallet.

Relax and take a few silent breaths, then focus your thoughts on the item you wish to locate. Visualize it in your mind.

Slowly and smoothly move around your house, watching the sharp end of the pencil. As you draw near the misplaced item, the point will dip down slightly. When you are very close to it, the pencil may dip so much that it falls from your hand. If so, just replace it and continue until you locate what you have lost.

If you do not have success on your first try, do not be discouraged. Remember, you are training your mind to receive and be aware of very subtle communications from a source that is outside your consciousness. This is something that must be learned.

You can experiment with other objects for your dowsing rod, such as a butter knife or a letter opener. You must be able to balance the rod across your index finger so that it can easily dip down. The finer this balance, the more sensitive the oracle. If you have no success using your left hand, try your right hand. Find the hand that works best for you.

Continue to practice in this way on a daily basis for at least several weeks. It only takes a few minutes of your time, but during those few minutes, you must be completely focused and aware of what you are doing.

Exercise 11.8: Automatic Drawing

Spirits sometimes find it easier to communicate with us through symbols and images instead of words. One way to achieve this communication is through what is called automatic drawing. A question is asked, and the spirit or spirits present are encouraged to use the hand of the channeler to give a response in the form of a drawing or drawings.

You do not have to possess artistic skill to use this method of channeling. Even if you are only able to draw stick figures, it is enough to convey useful information.

Six sheets of ordinary copier paper and a pencil are all that you need for this exercise. Number the sheets in the upper-right corner from one to six. Set the blank sheets of paper on a table and place a pencil beside them.

Automatic drawing allows you to ask complex or abstract questions, such as "What is the most important event that will happen to me next week?" or "What is my destiny?" or "How can I find happiness in my life?" The response will be derived by interpreting what you draw in a symbolic way.

Before you begin, you should loosen up your drawing arm and hand. For most people, this will be the right arm, but if you are left-handed, it will be the left. In a standing position, swing your arm around in large circles a dozen times, then reverse the direction of the circles. Shake your hand gently on the end of your wrist while holding your fingers loose.

Sit at the table and take up the pencil. On the sheet of paper numbered one, begin by drawing circles around and around, first in one direction, then the other. Change to jagged lines and make a dozen or so across the paper. Draw some undulating curves.

Keep your mind blank while doing this scribbling. Don't worry what these things look like or if they overlap on the paper. They are merely for the purpose of opening a channel between the spirit that will provide the response and your drawing hand.

Put aside the first sheet and lay the sheet numbered two in front of you. Write your question at the top of the sheet so that you will have a record of it, then ask the question out loud while gazing at the empty space on the sheet. While you are speaking, keep the question clearly in your mind and listen to your own voice speaking.

Immediately after voicing your question, relax and clear your mind completely. Take up the pencil and begin to doodle on the paper. Do not try to draw anything, and have no intention as you do this. Let your hand draw whatever lines and angles, whatever figures, whatever pictures it wishes to draw. It is important that you keep your mind empty. You can watch the doodling, but do not think about it or care about it. Do not help or hinder the drawings. Allow them to arise as they will.

When you fill up the sheet of paper, set it aside and do the same on the next sheet. If you wish, you can ask a separate question for each sheet. Or you can continue drawing on all six sheets for the same question. Write each question down so that you have a record if it. The numbering on the sheets allows you to keep them in their correct sequence after you end the exercise.

When you have filled all six sheets with doodling, set the pencil down, close your eyes, and take several silent breaths to end the exercise.

The results of automatic drawing must be interpreted symbolically in relation to the question asked. This is largely an intuitive process. When you study the drawings at a later time, you will see some features that stand out and seem more important than others. Try to connect them to aspects of the question. You may get such things as a heart, a snake, a dagger, a flower, geometric forms like a triangle or square, a bridge, a gateway, spirals, faces, buildings, animals, and so on. Also be aware of the relationship between one form with another on the paper. Some shapes will be bigger and others tiny; some will be at the top of the page and others at the bottom. Some may be overlapping, isolated from the rest, or even upside down.

Interpreting the results of automatic drawing is an art in itself. No one can do it for you. What you have drawn in direct response to your question will have more meaning for you than for anybody else. Do not throw the sheets away. In the days or weeks following the exercise, take them out every so often and study them for meaning.

Exercise 11.9: Deriving Sigils

By using the channeling method of automatic drawing, it is possible to derive the sigil of a spirit. In this exercise, you will invoke the spirit of the house or apartment in which you live and invite the spirit to convey its sigil to you.

Dim the lights slightly, but not so much that you cannot see. Sit at a table with a sheet of blank paper and a pencil. Take a few silent breaths to clear and focus your mind.

Press your palms together in front of your breast or, if you prefer, in front of your forehead in a gesture of prayer. Close your eyes and recite the words of this incantation or words of similar meaning:

Spirit of this dwelling place,
Close behind me stand;
Make your sigil known to me,
Spirit, guide my hand.

The incantation should be tailored to correspond with the spirit whose sigil you are seeking to obtain. It is helpful if you know the name of the spirit but not essential, provided you know some quality or aspect of the spirit that identifies it in your own thoughts. In the example used above, it is the spirit of your home. It could be the spirit of one of your ancestors or your family bloodline, a tree, a spring, or a familiar spirit you have summoned to perform specific tasks.

After you invoke and instruct the spirit, take up the pencil and open your mind. Allow the pencil to mark whatever pattern of lines arises automatically. Pretend that your hand has a life of its own. The spirit will guide it to draw its sigil. Spirit sigils are usually patterns of curves and angled lines that have no obvious pictorial meaning. They are graphic forms of the spirit's signature.

Whichever sigil you derive will be unique to you. It will serve you when you seek to summon or direct the spirit it identifies, but it will not serve any other person.

After your hand has drawn the sigil, thank the spirit for its presence and say goodbye to it. Put the sigil in a secure place until you wish to use it for communicating with that spirit or directing it to perform some task.

Exercise 11.10: Automatic Writing

Automatic writing requires more channeling ability than automatic drawing. By taking control of the channeler's hand and arm, a spirit is able to transmit information in the form of written words. This is more intellectual, less intuitive, than the transmission of images and patterns.

There are many degrees of proficiency to this skill, from the transmission of complete books suitable for publication down to individual words or even broken portions of words. Do not expect to be able to channel polished prose on the first few attempts. As is true of so many aspects of magic, automatic writing at a high level requires a natural gift that must be developed. Those without the gift will never become experts, but almost everyone can succeed to a useful degree with practice.

For this exercise, you will need half a dozen sheets of blank paper and a pencil. It is a good idea to number the sheets in the upper corner so that at a later time you will know their sequence. Sit at a table with these things in front of you and take a minute to draw a few silent breaths with your eyes shut to calm and focus before beginning.

Form a prayer gesture with your palms pressed together and speak the following brief incantation or words of the same purpose:

Spirits of the light,
Make your presence known.
Guide my hand aright;
Let your words be shown.

It is useful to have a question in mind to ask the spirits, as a way of focusing their attention on you. When you begin this exercise, you might ask, "Is there anything you wish me to know?" It is best to voice the question aloud. Write it down on the top of the first sheet of paper as well. You can try different questions to see which one the spirits will respond to, but only ask one question at each session.

With your eyes open, take up the pencil in your dominant hand and make a few rows of relaxed circles across the first sheet of paper. Then make a few rows of up-and-down zigzags. Keep your mind blank. Strive for an abstracted mental state—be aware of what you are doing, but do not be involved with it. Let your hand move by itself in whatever way it wants to move.

When you have loosened up your writing hand, begin making marks that resemble writing but are not actual writing. You may have seen young children do this when they imitate writing before actually learning how to write. Have the paper in your field of view, but do not focus strongly on it. You need just enough attention on the paper to avoid running off its edge.

If you prefer to block print rather than write with cursive script, imitate writing in block printing without actually writing anything.

Hold the pencil lightly and allow its point to glide across the sheet. Do not consciously or deliberately make any particular shapes, but allow the gibberish script to form itself from moment to moment.

I'm sure you have heard about Christians who speak in tongues. This is not speaking in any actual language but is the making of sounds that resemble some unknown tongue. Automatic writing is a kind of writing in tongues. At some point, a spirit will take partial control over your hand and cause you to make script or letters that are not random but carry meaning.

When the first sheet of paper is filled, set it aside and continue on the next sheet. Keep going until all six sheets are filled. Do not study what you have marked on the sheets while you are marking them. Do not look directly at your pencil point. It is best to keep your eyes focused on infinity, as though you were looking through the table into the infinite distance beneath it.

The exercise is over when all six sheets have been filled. Set down the pencil, close your eyes, and take several silent breaths to relax and return to your everyday state of mind.

At some later time, study the marks you have made on the sheets in detail, looking for any that are nonrandom. Some of them will be letters or parts of words. There may even be whole words and phrases mixed in among the gibberish false-writing. These will be communications from the spirit who guided your hand. As you progress with this exercise, it is likely that more actual written words or even whole sentences will appear.

Once you have a clear communication from a spirit, you should ask the spirit to give its name and to draw its sigil. In future communications with this spirit, invoke it by name and inscribe its name and sigil at the head of the first sheet of paper.

ASTRAL PROJECTION

Astral projection is the separation of the consciousness from the physical body. It occurs spontaneously, but can also be induced deliberately by those who have developed their natural talent for it. Few people can do astral projection at will. It is one of the rarest skills in Western magic. Those individuals with a gift for it find it possible to project astrally not only to any place on the surface of the earth but to any place in the universe and to higher dimensions of reality. These higher dimensions are sometimes referred to as the astral planes. They are the dwelling places of spirits.

Astral projection usually takes the form of the projection of an astral double of the physical body, which separates from the physical body while the physical body sits or lies in an unconscious state. However, it can also take the form of the projection of a bodiless point of consciousness that is able to move from place to place and observe events around it.

Those engaged in astral travel sometimes observe a shining cord attaching their astral body to their physical body. As they travel through the astral realms, this cord stretches. Its ability to stretch appears to be unlimited. It glows with a cool silvery whiteness that resembles moonlight. Not every astral traveler is aware of the existence of this silver cord.

All astral projection occurs on the astral level, as the very name itself implies. The lowest of the astral planes resembles our physical world very closely, so closely in fact that most people who project into it are under the mistaken belief that they have projected their astral bodies through physical space. This is inaccurate.

The lower astral plane is like a mirror for the physical plane that our bodies occupy. By traveling across the lower astral plane, it is possible to visit distant locations around the world and to observe what is taking place in those locations—but astral travelers are always moving on the astral plane and are observing events on the astral plane that mirror events in the physical world.

This is the reason that places visited during astral projection do not perfectly correspond with the physical locations they represent. The correspondence between the physical world and the lower astral plane can be very close, but the lower astral will always differ in small ways, or sometimes in larger ways, from the physical world.

A consequence of this aspect of astral travel is that events viewed during astral projection cannot be automatically assumed to have happened exactly as they were observed. When viewing some scene during astral travel, it is important not to jump to the conclusion that it corresponds with reality. It will often be indistinguishable from the actual events it represents, but sometimes it will differ from those events. The lower astral is a mirror of the physical plane, but it is an imperfect and inconstant reflection that can be distorted by the emotions and expectations of the astral traveler.

DREAMS

Dreams are a form of astral travel. During dreaming, the conscious mind is usually not in its normal state. It is uncritical of irrational sequences of events and will accept the most absurd happenings as natural. We have all experienced dreams in which absurd things occurred, but we did not realize they were absurd until after we awoke from sleep.

There may be a connection between the inability of the dreamer to reason during a dream and the tendency of spirits who communicate with human beings to have difficulty distinguishing truth from falsehood. The normal state of the human mind during dreams may approximate the mental condition of spiritual beings that dwell on the astral planes. When we dream, we become ourselves residents of the astral planes.

At rare intervals, we may regain full consciousness and become aware during a dream. We usually first assume that we are awake, until some small, incongruous detail of the dream reminds us that we are asleep and dreaming. This kind of dreaming with conscious awareness is called lucid dreaming, because the mind is clear and alert, with the ability to make sound judgments and distinguish fact from fiction.

There is no practical difference between astral projection and lucid dreaming. The reason these two activities are usually referred to as separate is the mistaken view that during astral projection, we actually project some part of ourselves through physical space. This never happens. All astral projection occurs on the astral planes—usually on the lowest astral plane, which very closely resembles the physical world.

The astral planes are a complex form of sensory metaphor. They are creations of our minds, but they are based on an underlying reality of a nature inaccessible to our physical senses. In order to allow our conscious awareness to perceive this reality, it is translated into sensory metaphors—into sights, sounds, touches, tastes, and odors. Our consciousness can only deal with sensory input, so if this translation were not made, we would have no awareness of the astral planes at all. It is a trick of our minds to allow us to be aware of information that transcends our senses, but it is not a lie—the astral planes are real.

We have a tendency to conflate the real with the physical. We tend to believe that if something isn't physical, it isn't real, and if it isn't real, it can't be physical. This is a natural error to make when we consider that our consciousness can only handle sensory data, and the physical senses transmit information only from the physical world. But thanks to sensory metaphors, our deep mind is able to convey information to our consciousness concerning levels of higher reality that are not physical in any way. We do this spontaneously during dreams, but sometimes we are able to do it deliberately during astral projection.

HOW TO FACILITATE ASTRAL PROJECTION

To create the best environment for astral projection, we should surround ourselves with sensory triggers linked to the moon. Colors of the moon are black, white, silver, and purple. The lunar metal is silver. Scents associated with this planet are heavy and stupefying, conducive to the induction of sleep, such as jasmine, rose, and opium. Scented candles or incense in the form of cones or sticks may be burned for this purpose. Music of the moon is instrumental, slow, dreamy, otherworldly. Crystals, mirrors, and vessels of clear water attract and concentrate lunar virtue. The presence of cats will help to induce a lunar atmosphere—cats are the most lunar of all animals.

It can be useful to observe astrological times when seeking to project into the astral planes. Monday is the day of the moon, and night is a better time for astral travel than day. At night the mind becomes receptive and the emotions are heightened. The best phase of the lunar cycle for astral projection is during the three nights when the orb of the moon shows a full disk, but the waxing phase when the moon approaches its fullness is also good.

Astral projection should be practiced either lying on your back or seated in a comfortable padded armchair. Silence is usually best, or as little background sound as possible, but you may wish to put on soft classical music as a way of masking low-level noises or as an aid in achieving the right frame of mind. If so, choose instrumental music that does not have sudden loud passages. Chamber music is a good type for this purpose. Stringed instruments are best—their sound is lunar.

The room should be warm enough that you will not become chilled and start to shiver, but not so hot that it is uncomfortable. Wear loose clothing or pajamas, and take off your shoes, belt, and any other items that constrict, such as a wristwatch or tie. Total darkness, or at least a dim light, will encourage success—darkness and shadows are of the moon.

There is no guarantee that the exercises at the end of this chapter will enable you to do astral projection at will. That is a very rare talent. However, regular and persistent practice of them will develop your occult abilities in the area of astral perception and astral manipulation and will facilitate your natural gift for traveling on the astral planes, if such a gift is innately yours.

EXERCISES FOR CHAPTER 12

Exercise 12.1: Phantom Hand

Astral projection involves the separation of the astral body from the physical body. Although this occurs on the astral level, it appears to happen on the physical level. When you separate from your body, it seems to you that you are actually leaving your physical body.

This exercise will develop your ability to separate your astral arm from your physical arm. You will need a silver or glass bowl filled with ice water. Put a few ice cubes into the water to keep it cold during the practice session.

Place the bowl of ice water on the edge of a table and sit in front of it in the sitting posture, with your hands resting on your knees and your feet flat on the floor. You must be near enough to the bowl to reach out and easily touch it with your right hand.

We will use the right arm for this exercise because the right side of the body is the side that normally projects. If you are left-handed, you may wish to do the exercise with your left hand, since this will be your dominant hand.

Take several silent breaths to focus on what you are about to do. Gaze at the bowl of water, and at the same time, shift your awareness to your right hand, which is resting on your right knee. Be totally conscious of your right hand, the way your fingers are curved over your knee, the touch of the cloth covering your knee or your skin if your knee is bare, the tiny currents of air that stir the little hairs on the back of your hand.

Allow your awareness to extend from your right hand over your wrist, along your forearm, around your bent elbow, and up your upper arm to your right shoulder. Hold the awareness of your entire right arm clearly in your mind.

Close your eyes. Take a deep breath, hold it for a beat, then exhale slowly and audibly from your pursed lips. As you exhale, without moving your physical hand from your knee, lift your astral hand and arm, extend them forward, and lower your astral hand into the ice water.

Feel, as clearly as you can visualize it, the sudden shock of the cold water around your fingers and hand as you lower your astral hand into the water. Take care not to tense up the physical muscles of your hand and arm—keep them completely relaxed and motionless. You are moving your astral hand, not your physical hand.

Hold your astral hand in the water for half a dozen seconds, then draw it out and return it to your right knee. Open your eyes and look at the bowl of ice water. Take several silent breaths.

Repeat this procedure of closing your eyes and extending your astral hand into the water, then withdrawing it and replacing it on your knee, three times. Do not rush. Give yourself a chance to fully be aware of your hand and arm, as well as time to experience the chillness of the ice water on your astral fingers as you submerge them.

To end, open your eyes and take a few silent breaths.

Exercise 12.2: Stepping Out

It is helpful to dim the lights or draw the curtains to create an artificial twilight. Stand facing east with your arms at your sides. Take a few silent breaths to focus your mind.

Be aware of your body. Extend your spine upward from your heels to straighten it, and stretch upward with the top of your head, as though a string were attached to your skull and pulling gently upward. Do not strain your muscles, but be conscious of them. At the same time, flatten your hands and extend your arms downward gently, then relax them.

Close your eyes. Take a deep breath, hold it for a beat, then exhale slowly and audibly. As you exhale, take one step backward onto your left foot with your astral body, separating it from your physical body. Do not move your physical body as you do this. In your astral body, stand with arms at your sides, and in your mind, see your physical body in front of you. See the back of your head, your neck, your shoulders. Look down the length of your physical body to your heels, then back up to your head as you draw several silent breaths.

Take one step forward onto your right foot with your astral body to bring it back into your physical body, and feel it enter your body through your clothing and the barrier of your skin. Feel your muscles and bones. Feel the warmth of your blood on your astral body.

Open your eyes and take a few silent breaths. You can repeat this procedure several times during your exercise. Pause between repetitions to allow enough time to elapse so that you are fully aware of your physical body before stepping out of it.

To end, open your eyes after your final repetition and take several silent breaths to relax.

Exercise 12.3: Remote Viewing

Remote viewing may not seem like a form of astral travel, but when you remote view, you project your bodiless awareness across the lower astral plane and observe events there that correspond with events occurring in the same location in the physical world.

Before beginning the exercise, you must have a target destination in mind. You can use a place with which you are personally familiar, such as your family home or vacation cabin, or you can use a famous location such as the Taj Mahal in India or the Grand Canyon.

It is helpful to have a photograph of the target destination, and spend ten minutes or so contemplating it before beginning, so that it will be clear in your mind.

You can do this exercise sitting in a chair or lying on your back. I suggest that you use a comfortable padded armchair so that you can remain relaxed for an extended period without needing to concentrate on your physical posture. The practice room should be quiet, the lighting dimmed.

Sit in the armchair and lean back to relax. Rest your hands on the arms of the chair or in your lap, whichever feels more comfortable. Take several silent breaths. Close your eyes.

Inhale deeply, hold it for a beat, then exhale audibly through your pursed lips as you project your point of view forward and outward from your body in a great rush to the location you have previously contemplated. Visualize your awareness flashing forward at great speed, so that all you can see is a blur on all sides, until you find yourself in the target location.

Be aware of the location site all around you, but do not visualize your body. Remain only a floating point of awareness as you gaze around at the location you have selected and as you move through it, observing it as you go.

It is important in this exercise not to force the visualization but to open yourself to visual perceptions of the place to which you have projected your awareness. You know more or less what it looks like from your contemplation of it, but allow details to arise spontaneously while you are there. Allow yourself to be surprised by what you see. Simply observe events as they unfold. Continue in this way for ten minutes or so.

To return to your body, shift your awareness from the target location back to your physical body. Be aware of the chair pressing against your back and legs. Be aware of your posture. Your awareness of these physical perceptions will return with a rush as your consciousness reenters your flesh.

Open your eyes and take a few silent breaths to calm and relax your mind and end the exercise.

Exercise 12.4: Lucid Dreaming

The difficulty in practicing the technique of lucid dreaming is that it only happens when you become aware that you are in a dream, and when you are in a dream, you almost never know it until after it is over. Even so, it is possible to create a symbolic trigger that may help you become conscious that you are dreaming during the dream itself.

Find a rounded, flat stone that fits easily into your hand when you close your fingers around it. The stone should be smooth, with no rough corners or edges, and around two inches across. On one side of this stone, paint the astrological symbol of the sun with gold paint—this symbol is a circle with a dot in its center. On the other side, paint the symbol of an open eye using sky-blue paint.

Usually when we deal with astral perception, we use the symbolism of the moon. But in this exercise, we seek to attain self-awareness within our dreams, and consciousness is a quality of the sun. That is why a sun symbol is painted on the stone rather than the symbol of the moon.

When you go to bed for the night, lie on your back with this stone resting on your forehead between and just above your eyebrows with the blue, open eye facing upward. Spend several minutes meditating on the shining disk of the sun. Visualize its brightness, its golden rays beaming down through clouds, its red disk rising in the early morning and flooding the eastern sky with rosy light. When your mind is filled with the sun, recite the following incantation:

Mighty Helios, source of light,
Fill my mind and grant me sight.
When all is not just as it seems,
Light my way in lands of dreams.

Take the stone off your forehead and hold it in your left hand, which is your hand of reception. Go to sleep with the stone held loosely in your left fist.

When you begin to dream, remember the stone. In the dream, become aware that it is in your hand. Tighten your fingers around it. The touch of the stone in your dream will cause you to regain your awareness and realize that you are dreaming.

This trigger to initiate lucid dreaming is not infallible, but it can be effective if you link your thoughts to the stone, and to the radiance of the sun that it symbolizes, just prior to drifting off to sleep, and if you keep the stone in your left hand. The light of the sun represents self-awareness.

Exercise 12.5: Levitation

Lie on your back on your bed in the dark. Take a few silent breaths to focus on what you are about to do. Close your eyes.

Become aware of your body. Perform the stepped relaxation you learned in the first exercise of chapter 3 (page 40). Concentrate on your legs and deliberately relax them by withdrawing your consciousness from them, then your arms, then your stomach, then your chest and shoulders, then your head. Draw your awareness into a point in the center of your head and imagine yourself bodiless.

Visualize yourself lying on your back on a raft in the warm southern ocean. The ocean swell lifts the raft gently upward, then after a moment drops it gently downward, so that as it falls you feel a kind of thrill, the same sensation you get in an elevator when it starts to drop. It is not frightening. The slow rhythm of rise and fall is soothing and relaxing.

Concentrate only on the sensation of dropping into the trough in the ocean swell and sustain it, so that the dropping sensation does not stop but continues. Sustain this feeling of gently falling or dropping away in your body. Become aware that there is nothing beneath you. You are falling slowly and gently because there is nothing to hold you up. The sensation of the water falling away beneath you will encourage the separation of your astral body from your physical body.

When you have a sense of this separation, visualize your consciousness in your astral body rising three or four feet above your physical body on the bed. Let your physical body drop away beneath you as you rise into the darkness. Feel the separation between your astral form, which holds your awareness, and your physical form so far below as you drift up and up through the night.

When you feel that you have risen as high as you can, return your awareness to your physical body and reintegrate your astral shell with it. Open your eyes and take a few silent breaths to end the exercise.

Exercise 12.6: Astral Penetration

Adopt the sitting posture at a table. Rest your right hand on the table but keep your left hand on your left knee. Take a few silent breaths to prepare your mind.

Close your eyes. Transfer your awareness into your right hand and forearm, where they touch the surface of the table. Feel the hardness of the table under your hand. Do not press down or move your hand; merely feel the touch of the table against it.

Visualize your right hand and arm passing slowly downward through the table. Do not move your physical arm, but separate an astral arm from your physical arm and lower the astral arm through the table.

The sensation of your astral body penetrating physical objects is quite distinctive. You will know it when you feel it. There is a slight resistance, then your astral form seems to slide or filter through the material surface like water passing through a window screen. Visualize your astral body sliding between the molecules of the table.

Lower your astral right hand to your right knee and rest it there, while keeping your awareness detached from your physical right hand, still lying on the surface of the table. Be aware of your physical left hand on your left knee and the similar sensation of your astral right hand on your right knee. Hold this awareness in your mind for a minute or two.

To end the exercise, shift your awareness to your physical right hand and arm, and put your physical right hand on your right knee, superimposing it on your astral right hand. Open your eyes and take a few silent breaths to end the exercise.

Exercise 12.7: Silver Cord Awareness

Not everyone who projects on the astral planes is aware of their silver cord, which links their astral body to their physical body while the two are separated. Even so, the silver cord is always there, because there is always a connection between the astral body and the physical body. The two only fully separate at death.

The awareness of the silver cord is a sensory metaphor by which the conscious mind is made able to consider something real that exists but that lies beyond the reach of the senses and beyond the conception of normal consciousness. It is a translation of what cannot be conceived into a metaphorical form that can be held in the awareness and considered. For this reason, details of the nature of the silver cord will differ from one person to another, just as descriptions of the aura differ.

In this exercise, you will practice becoming aware of the link between your physical form and your projected astral form.

Stand in the standing posture facing east, and take a few silent breaths. Close your eyes.

Become aware of your body. Hold your entire body awareness in your mind from the soles of your feet to the crown of your head. Draw a deep, silent breath through your nose, and release a slow, audible breath between your lips as you turn your astral self counterclockwise 180 degrees without moving your physical body. Rotate your astral body to the left so that you face behind yourself, while still standing inside your physical body. Keep your awareness focused on your astral body, and do not tense your physical muscles.

Slowly take a step backward in your astral body so that you separate from your physical body and stand face-to-face with your physical body. Even though your physical eyelids are closed, you can see yourself with your astral eyes, which are open. Look at your physical body standing directly in front of your astral form.

Take another step backward with your astral body and stand still, gazing back at your physical body. Become aware of a shining elastic connection between your abdomen where your navel is located and the abdomen of your physical body. It is around three inches thick and glows as though lit by moonlight. This same glow surrounds both your physical body and your astral body.

Step back a third time and watch this silvery cord stretch and become thinner, like a band of silvery elastic. Be aware of the slight pulling sensation it produces on your lower abdomen. It is a very gentle tug.

To conclude the exercise, step forward three steps into your physical body, so that your astral shell merges with your physical shell. You are still facing the wrong way. Take a deep breath, and exhale audibly while rotating your astral body clockwise so that it faces in the same direction as your physical body.

Open your eyes and draw several silent breaths, then go about your day.

Exercise 12.8: Remote Visitation

Although astral travel occurs on the astral level, it is possible for other human beings to become aware of your astral body when it is present near them. This occurs most often with those you know well and with whom you have a close emotional bond, such as a friend or family member.

It occurs spontaneously when people die. A member of the family or a close friend will report seeing the deceased standing before them at the time of death, even though they were physically many miles away at that moment. The trauma of dying causes them to spontaneously project their astral forms to the awareness of those they love.

It is possible to do the same thing deliberately. In this exercise, you will practice projecting your astral double to a person you know well who is emotionally close to you. It is best done late at night, after you have gone to bed.

Lie on your back in your bed and close your eyes. Allow yourself time to fully relax. Think of the person you wish to appear before. Visualize them lying asleep in their own bed in their house or apartment. If you know what their bedroom looks like, so much the better, but if not, just visualize them lying in a bed asleep.

Feel yourself in your astral body, standing beside their bed in the dark as you gaze down upon the person who lies sleeping. Listen to the soft sounds of that person's breaths.

Reach out and gently brush your fingertips over the forehead and cheek of the sleeper. Keep doing this until the person opens his or her eyes and looks at you. Smile gently and nod your head when they see you.

Shift your awareness back to your body in your own bed. Your projected astral form will snap back into your body. Be aware of your own body for a minute or so, then let yourself fall asleep.

Do not tell what you have done to the person who was the target for this exercise. If they mention that they were thinking of you in the night, dreamed about you, or thought they saw you in the darkness of their bedroom, it will be confirmation of your progress in astral projection, but even if they give no indication that they were thinking about you, the exercise is valuable for developing your skill in astral projection.

Exercise 12.9: Astral Messaging

When you wish to convey a message to another person, you can do so by projecting your astral body to that person and whispering the message into their ear. The best time to do this is when the person is asleep and their mind is open and receptive. The message should be kept short and the wording simple. A brief, direct statement has the best chance of being remembered after the recipient wakes up.

Lie on your bed at a time when you know the person you are targeting will be asleep. Take several silent breaths to prepare and focus your mind. Know the message you intend to convey and hold it in the back of your mind. Close your eyes.

Become aware of your body on the bed. Relax completely, and withdraw your awareness from your body to the center of your head. Without moving your physical body in any way, sit up and then stand beside your bed. Do this almost without thinking, in an automatic way. Be aware of your astral body standing beside the bed with your back turned on your physical body. Do not turn around to look at yourself.

Picture in your mind the person with whom you seek to communicate. Visualize that person lying in bed asleep. Allow your astral body to lean forward and rush through space to where the other person lies sleeping. This feels like zooming through a tunnel at incredible speed so that everything flashes past on all sides. It's something like warp drive in Star Trek or in the Star Wars movies.

Look down at the sleeping person. Lean down and hold your lips close to the person's ear. With your astral body, speak the message you desire to convey to that person clearly into their ear. Do not move your physical lips or speak out loud as you do this. All your awareness should be on your astral body and the room where the person lies sleeping.

To return to your physical body, imagine yourself inside your physical body on your own bed. Become aware of the sensations of your body. Open your eyes and take several silent breaths to end the exercise.

The person to whom you communicated your message may or may not speak to you about it at a later date. Even if they do not speak of it, the message will have seated itself in their subconscious mind. They will believe it to be their own thoughts when it occurs to their conscious awareness and will act on it as they would act on their own thoughts. This is a useful method for influencing the actions of others. It should never be used in a malicious way, but only to comfort or help others.

Exercise 12.10: Astral Flight

When you travel through the astral planes, you are not limited to walking. You can move across the planes without a body, as no more than an observing point of view; or, if you wish, you can flash your point of awareness almost instantly to any location you conceptualize. But there is another way to travel the astral realms—you can fly like a bird.

Everyone has had dreams of flying. It is one of the more common types of dreams. You glide off the ground and ascend to whatever elevation you wish to attain, or at least to whatever elevation you feel comfortable with sustaining, passing over trees and rooftops.

You can practice astral flight in your imagination. This practice is useful as a way of learning how to project your point of view outside your physical body and will enable you to fly with confidence when you find yourself projected onto the astral planes, either in your dreams or deliberately while you are still awake.

This exercise is best done at night, just before you go to sleep. It is an exercise in visualization, but it can become more than this. Visualization can be used to prime the pump of astral projection.

Lie on your back on your bed. Take a few silent breaths to relax your body and prepare your mind. Close your eyes.

Visualize your astral body becoming lighter and lighter. Think of it as hollow, no heavier than a soap bubble. Imagine it gently rising off the bed. Feel the bed drop away beneath you as you float free of your physical body and start to rise into the air.

Be aware that there is something pulling you upward the way a magnet attracts iron. Feel this pull all over the surface of your astral body. It is the stars that attract you. They draw you upward with their connecting rays, which converge all over your body like countless invisible wires. Individually, the attraction of each ray is weak, but together all the rays from the stars lift you irresistibly up to press against your ceiling.

Will your astral body to pass through the molecules of your ceiling and farther on up through the roof of your building into the open night air. Your astral body slides through the spaces between the physical particles that make up the ceiling and roof with only a slight resistance that you can feel as you pass through. It is a strange but not an unpleasant feeling, a kind of soft, yielding resistance that gives way and closes behind you.

Allow the attraction of the stars to continue to pull you upward into the sky. Turn your body to look down at the ground as it recedes below you. See the houses and streets, the cars and trees, becoming smaller.

When you are high enough to be free of terrestrial obstructions, use the power of your will to stop your upward progress. You will still feel the pull of the stars, but you can resist it. Cause your astral body to glide forward across the landscape while you watch it pass below you. It is what an owl sees when it glides silently above the trees through the darkness. The streetlights and the lights of windows pass below you.

Fly in your imagination over the rooftops and the treetops for as long as you wish, but when you become tired, direct your astral body back to your own home and use the power of your will to gently push it down through the roof and through the ceiling into your bedroom. As you do this, turn your astral body so that you are horizontal and facing upward. Gently press your astral body back into your physical body, which lies motionless below you on the bed.

When you feel yourself once more a part of your physical body, move your arms and legs to stretch them. Open your eyes and take a few deliberate silent breaths. Roll over and go to sleep to end the exercise.

AFTERWORD
WALK YOUR OWN PATH

In seeking to study so vast and varied a subject as magic, it's easy to become discouraged. Early successes can be thrilling, even intoxicating. They carry us up to dizzying heights of expectation. But when they are followed by failure after failure, the tendency is to lose hope and stop practicing.

It is a recognized phenomenon in magic that beginners often achieve astonishing results the first time they try a technique, then find that their success diminishes on subsequent attempts. For example, the first time they work the Ouija board, they may get instant spirit communications of a startling kind. Later, when they try to duplicate these results, they cannot do it. This has been noted in the field of paranormal research as well. A psychic may have a high accuracy rate on the Zener cards the first time they are read, and then may see this accuracy drop on later readings. Gamblers call this beginner's luck. Don't try to tell gamblers that it is only imagination or coincidence. They know better.

It's important not to give up during periods when your attempts to work magic seem to make no progress at all or when they seem to even regress. By this I mean, at times you may find that doing magic not only fails to achieve your goals but actually makes things worse! This can be very disheartening, but you must not lose heart. Remember, you are building up your mental body by doing these exercises, just as a weightlifter builds up the physical body by lifting weights. At times, you will feel weaker, and at other times, you will feel stronger. This is a natural part of the process of occult psychic development. You are exercising powers of your mind that under normal circumstances are almost never used. It takes time and consistent practice to master them.

As you continue to practice over a span of months, you will feel the effect of your work as physical changes in your brain and nervous system. This can be quite startling. It certainly startled me when I first noticed that I was feeling changes inside my skull, actual physical changes. Under normal conditions, you don't feel your brain at all unless you get a headache, but these exercises will cause new pathways to be formed in your brain, and you will feel these pathways as they develop. You will also feel changes to your nerves throughout your body. Don't worry—it is not a painful feeling, but it will be strange to you, because it will be something you have never felt before.

Consistency is really the key to any process of self-improvement, physical or mental. Practice daily. Never strain your body or mind during practice. Use a sustained, mild pressure of the will to achieve progress. The easiest way to become discouraged and give up is to try to force matters with an intense effort of will and, when success is not achieved, to give up in anger and despair and stop practice entirely.

This is the meaning to the saying "Slow and steady wins the race." Be steady in your practice so that you see a little progress when you look back across a month of exercises, and take it slow so that you do not exhaust yourself and fall into a state of depression. If you persist in this way, slow and steady, you will win out over others who at first glance seem to be more naturally gifted for magic than you. Natural gifts are wonderful to have, but they can only take you so far. In the end, you must rely on training, conditioning, and self-discipline. Coupled with natural gifts, which we all possess to some degree, these ensure consistent success in the long term.

BIBLIOGRAPHY

Agrippa, Cornelius. *Three Books of Occult Philosophy.* Edited by Donald Tyson. St. Paul, MN: Llewellyn Publications, 1993.

Apuleius. *On the God of Socrates.* In *The Works of Apuleius*. London: H. G. Bohn, 1853.

Aubrey, John. *Miscellanies.* London, 1696.

Budge, E. A. Wallis. *Egyptian Magic.* Vol. 2, *Books on Egypt and Chaldea.* London: Kegan Paul, Trench, Trübner & Co., 1901.

Budge, E. A. Wallis, trans. and ed. *The History of Alexander the Great, Being the Syriac Version of the Pseudo-Callisthenes.* Cambridge, UK: Cambridge University Press, 1889.

Crowley, Aleister. *The Book of the Law*. South Stukely, Quebec: 93 Publishing, 1975.

Frazer, James George. *The Golden Bough*. Abr. ed. New York: Macmillan, 1927.

Leadbeater, Charles W. *Man Visible and Invisible: Examples of Different Types of Men as Seen by Means of Trained Clairvoyance.* 2nd ed. London: Theosophical Publishing House, 1920.

Pliny the Elder. *The Natural History of Pliny*. 6 vols. Translated by John Bostock and H. T. Riley. London: Henry G. Bohn, 1855–57.

Plutarch. *Plutarch's Morals.* 5 vols. Boston: Little, Brown, and Company, 1871–78.

Regardie, Israel. *The Golden Dawn*. 6th ed. St. Paul, MN: Llewellyn Publications, 1990.

Regardie, Israel. *The Middle Pillar*. 3rd ed. St. Paul, MN: Llewellyn Publications, 1998.

Roberts, Jane. *Seth Speaks: The Eternal Validity of the Soul*. Englewood Cliffs, NJ: Prentice-Hall, 1972.

Shakespeare, William. *Macbeth*. Edited by K. Deighton. London: Macmillan, 1891.

Sibly, Ebenezer. *A New and Complete Illustration of the Celestial Science of Astrology*. 13th ed. London: 1826.

INDEX OF EXERCISES

C

D

E

V

W

TO WRITE TO THE AUTHOR

If you wish to contact the author or would like more information about this book, please write to the author in care of Llewellyn Worldwide Ltd. and we will forward your request. Both the author and the publisher appreciate hearing from you and learning of your enjoyment of this book and how it has helped you. Llewellyn Worldwide Ltd. cannot guarantee that every letter written to the author can be answered, but all will be forwarded. Please write to:

Donald Tyson
℅ Llewellyn Worldwide
2143 Wooddale Drive
Woodbury, MN 55125-2989

Please enclose a self-addressed stamped envelope for reply, or $1.00 to cover costs. If outside the U.S.A., enclose an international postal reply coupon.

Many of Llewellyn's authors have websites with additional information and resources. For more information, please visit our website at https://www.llewellyn.com.

Notes

Notes

Notes

Notes